**What if** you could be happier, right now, without radically changing your life? As nationally recognized happiness expert Nataly Kogan teaches, happiness is not a nice feeling or a frivolous extra. It's a critical ingredient for living a fulfilling, meaningful, and healthy life—and it's a skill we can all learn and improve through practice. In *Happier Now,* Nataly shares an inspiring, science-based guide to help you build your happier skills and live with more joy, starting now.

Nataly's own journey from Russian refugee to founder and CEO of Happier taught her an important lesson: no matter how much you accomplish, how much you live the "right" way, or even how much gratitude you practice, life won't always be smooth. "We experience genuine and lasting happiness when we stop trying to turn the negative into the positive," Nataly writes, "and when we embrace the full range of our human emotions with compassion and strength."

*continued on back flap*

# Praise for *Happier Now*

"In *Happier Now*, Nataly Kogan traces her own journey to everyday happiness. What she discovers is that chasing one big goal rarely brings an end to self-doubt, fear, and unhappiness. Instead, true satisfaction is more often found in facing our negative emotions, cultivating self-care, and finding purpose in life. This book can be a guide to a life of genuine happiness."

DANIEL H. PINK
author of *Drive* and *A Whole New Mind*

"*Happier Now* will feed your soul and nourish your mind. Expect inspiration, practical advice, and greater confidence that true, lasting happiness is within reach."

ELENA BROWER
author of *Practice You*

"By synthesizing a treasure trove of psychology, neuroscience, and behavioral economics research, Nataly has created an immensely practical approach of what we can do every day to create more joy, feel more gratitude, and be happier. This is a book we can all learn from—no matter what our baseline levels of serotonin!"

BOB KOCHER, MD
former special assistant for health-care and economic policy for President Obama; adjunct professor, Stanford University; and partner at Venrock

"Through doable, accessible practices, Nataly teaches us how to find joy in everyday moments—rather than hanging our happiness on the next big milestone—and how to avoid being guided by our ego and remember that we're a being, not a doing. As a mom, my biggest takeaway was the importance of teaching my kids that it's okay to not be happy sometimes instead of giving them a distraction to make them happy."

**FRAN HAUSER**
startup investor, former president of digital at
Time Inc., and author of *The Myth of the Nice Girl*

"Nataly rocks! Her journey is not only honest and vulnerable but also practical and inspiring—no easy feat! *Happier Now* isn't your standard cliché-filled slog. Instead, it's a refreshing, insightful, and actionable guide to making small changes that add up to a more resilient and joyful life."

**DEREK FLANZRAICH**
CEO and founder of Greatist

"What I love about Nataly's book is that she challenges us all to forgive ourselves for saying 'I'll be happier when . . .' and instead start telling ourselves 'I'm happier because . . .' Gratitude is a strategy. This realization has helped me in my life, and I know it will help you, too."

**AMY JO MARTIN**
entrepreneur & *New York Times* bestselling author

"Nataly Kogan shows us that being happier isn't easy, but it is doable—and *Happier Now* offers insight into how to get there."

**MICHAEL NORTON**
coauthor of *Happy Money: The Science of Happier Spending*

"Every person on planet Earth wants the same thing—happiness. And yet it eludes most of us. With a skillful blend of scientific research and inspiring stories, Nataly teaches us that the keys to happiness are right in our hands."

BERT JACOBS
cofounder of Life is Good and
coauthor of *Life is Good: The Book*

"Nataly Kogan has a profound insight: that happiness is not just a feeling but something that we can practice. *Happier Now* is chock full of both the philosophy and tools we all need to transform and enrich the way we think about our lives—an invaluable resource for turbulent times."

DIANE HESSAN
entrepreneur, researcher, and CEO of Salient Ventures

"Part touching memoir, part practical workbook, *Happier Now* leads the reader on an entertaining and useful journey to increase life's joy and meaning."

ALEX KORB, PHD
author of *The Upward Spiral: Using Neuroscience to Reverse the Course of Depression, One Small Change at a Time*

"This book, like Nataly herself, is a shining beacon if you are at a point of absolute exhaustion or crisis in your life. Serving as your trusted guide, Nataly's road-tested wisdom will lead you into a deeply personal awakening and a happier, more fulfilling life. If you believe in 'signs,' then noticing this book at this exact point in YOUR life means that it was meant for YOU. Pick it up. Apply its lessons. Emerge *Happier Now*."

AMY GRAY
New Leaf Speaker Management

happier
now

# happier now

## How to Stop Chasing Perfection and Embrace Everyday Moments

### (Even the Difficult Ones)

## NATALY KOGAN

sounds true
BOULDER, COLORADO

Sounds True
Boulder, CO 80306

Published 2018

Cover design by Rachael Murray
Book design by Beth Skelley

Printed in Canada

Cataloging-in-Publication data for this book is available
from the Library of Congress

ISBN (hardcover): 978-1-68364-110-0
ISBN (ebook): 978-1-68364-155-1

10 9 8 7 6 5 4 3 2 1

For my Mia.
I love you
more
always.

# Contents

# Practices

# Gratitudes

To my parents, my heroes, my most amazing humans—thank you for you. None of this incredible, difficult, beautiful journey would be possible without you, your love, your care, your courage, your being. This book in its entirety is my letter of gratitude and love for you. I've been lucky to grow up with four loving grandparents, and I'm deeply grateful to my grandpa Misha, without whom we would not have dared to begin our journey to the United States, and to my grandmas Mirra and Sarra, and grandpa Sasha, who are no longer with us but are always in my heart.

I'm so grateful to Jaime Schwalb at Sounds True for nurturing this book—and me—with such tender care and passion. Thank you for believing in my voice before I did. Thank you to the entire team at Sounds True for your creativity, tenacity, and working like true partners through every step of creating and bringing this book to life.

Joelle Hann, my incredible editor, I'm eternally grateful for your wisdom, insight, and the kindness of your guidance. You have been an invaluable partner in helping bring my best self to write the best version of this book.

Thank you to my fearless agent, Janis Donnaud, for sticking with me and making sure we found the best home for this book. I am grateful for your tenacity and always looking out for me.

A huge thank you to the Happier team, past and present, close and far, for your hard work and dedication to bringing our mission of helping millions of people cultivate their happier skills. To everyone who has supported me on this quest, including our investors, advisors, and friends—thank you for being part of the most meaningful and unexpected journey of my life.

I wish I could give an enormous, larger-than-life hug to the Happier community and all the kind souls who have inspired, supported, and encouraged me through the years and continue to do so every day. This book isn't mine alone—it's ours, together. Thank you for your courage not only to be real and to be okay with not always being okay, but also to fight for moments of joy and beauty and kindness.

My deepest gratitude to the many people who generously shared their stories for this book. Some of you are dear friends, others I've never met in person, but you have all enriched this book by sharing parts of yourself—and helped to inspire many by doing so.

When the student is ready the teacher will appear. This was true in my case. Janet, my teacher and spiritual guide, I'm so grateful for your acceptance and invaluable guidance. I hope I honored your wisdom in this book; I continue to cherish it daily. I have also been incredibly lucky to learn from so many amazing yoga teachers—my soul sister Joanna, JoJo, Larissa, Elena, David, Amy, and many more. Thank you for your dedication in sharing yourselves and this sacred tradition, which has become my life's anchor. And without listing them all, I want to offer my deepest gratitude to the many teachers whose words have helped guide me, even though I've never met them.

My dear Sharon, thank you for your friendship, for flying with me to catch the rainbow, and for catching me when I fall. Thank you for seeing my true self before I had the courage to allow it to emerge.

The journey that led to this book began almost thirty years ago, and for twenty of those years I've walked this path with Avi, my husband, my partner, my greatest supporter, my love.

I don't have the words to express my gratitude to you for holding my hand through this rocky, amazing, scary, incredible adventure, for believing in me when I wanted to give up, for making me smile, for reading endless drafts, and for wrapping me with your kindness when the world was too harsh. I love you for always.

My Mia, my most amazing, dearest, magical human. This book is for you and because of you. Thank you for being the light on this journey, for being my staunch supporter, and for your invaluable help with the bibliography. But most of all, thank you for your being. I love you, more.

None of what we do, we do alone, and I'm grateful for the energy, the spirit, the beauty that is this life force that is within and surrounds us.

And finally, I offer my gratitude to you, my dear readers, for joining me on this journey. Knowing that this book might help another person find more moments of joy and weather life's storms with strength and compassion has been the bridge of resilience that carried me through my own storms as I wrote it.

# Introduction

I sat on the steps outside my company's office, leaning against the brick wall. It was a chilly October night. I wasn't wearing a jacket but I didn't feel cold—even though I'm always cold. It was around two in the morning. I didn't have a clue as to how long I had been sitting there or where I needed to be.

Our launch of Happier had been going extremely well. It had been a year of very hard work to bring our app—"A Social Network Dedicated to Happy Moments," as the *New York Times* called it—to life. Happier was a place for people to share little moments they were grateful for, no matter how small. I knew that gratitude worked (based on mountains of scientific research). It had helped me shift from always trying to chase happiness through hard work and achievements to being able to experience the many moments of joy, kindness, and beauty that were already present in my life. Happier mattered to me like no other company I had launched or worked at. It was born not just from an idea but also from my own struggles to feel content, to be in peaceful agreement with my life rather than constantly pushing and battling it.

I had a deep sense of gratitude for the great team of people who made the app and the launch happen, for having investors, friends, and family who had supported us. And there was so much to celebrate. Enthusiastic users. Fan mail telling us how lives were changed by using Happier. Invitations to exclusive conferences, speaking engagements, and lots of great press. It was the best a start-up could hope for at this early stage, and I knew it.

So why was I sliding into a total meltdown at work, at home, and in every part of my life? Why were strangers asking me if I was all right as I stood frozen in stores, on streets, or inches away from the subway tracks? Why did my daughter, who meant the world to me, and my husband, who was my rock, seem as if they were avoiding me? Why did I wake up every morning with an intense feeling of dread? Nothing made sense. I had realized my American dream for which I had worked so hard. I had broken through barrier after barrier in my life, outdoing myself with each one, and Happier was my crowning achievement. Ever since my parents and I came to the United States as refugees from former Soviet Russia, I had felt an intense desire to prove that the hardship of our immigration was worth it. Now that I had worked so hard and achieved so much, I should have been feeling ease, contentment, peace, and abundant happiness, all of which I was certain was on the other side of my achievements.

But it wasn't happening. I wasn't floating on cloud nine of never-ending amazing joy. Not even close. After the big—huge—achievement of the Happier launch, something vital was missing. Without it, I felt as if I couldn't breathe. It was something I had come to depend on with every major milestone, from learning to speak English without a Russian accent, to getting into a top college, to getting rare and coveted jobs at a young age—that feeling of elation. I didn't feel elated. I did for a little while, only to have an odd and uncomfortable feeling rise from deep in my stomach to replace it. Instead of escaping the tight grips of insecurity, anxiety, and fear that had accompanied me on our immigration so long ago, I was starting to drown in these feelings. I couldn't find the relief I had come to expect from another great performance.

It's normal when launching a start-up to go obsessively over and over terrible "what if . . . ?" scenarios, imagining immediate and total catastrophes. Every entrepreneur knows that a good launch doesn't end the stress of building a company from scratch. But this was more. I had begun to exist in a painfully divided state where I felt almost catatonic from worrying and stressing out about the company. At the same time, a voice in my head turned up the mean and negative dial to full volume: YOU'RE OBVIOUSLY NO GOOD AS AN ENTREPRENEUR! AND YOU'RE BEING A TERRIBLE MOM, WIFE, DAUGHTER, FRIEND, AND HUMAN BEING. YOU'RE JUST A FAILURE, THAT'S ALL!

I was caught in an exquisitely personal and extremely vicious cycle of self-doubt.

I knew burnout. I had experienced burnout before, a few years ago when I was a new mother, a managing director at a venture capital firm, running a publishing company from my kitchen table, and under contract to write an advice book. I felt desperate to find a way to feel better, and that is when I immersed myself in researching happiness, reading hundreds of studies. Surely someone else knew the answer already. I didn't. I had worked as hard as I could, leaping from one peak experience to another, and I still couldn't find the kind of happiness that lasted.

At first I rejected what I read—it couldn't be *that* simple—but the research was very convincing. So I started, albeit reluctantly, to practice gratitude. To my shock, it had a huge impact almost overnight. It turned even a hard-core skeptic like me into a believer. It was from that research and my desire to share this amazingly simple practice that was changing my life that Happier was born.

But now that Happier existed I could hardly function. Gratitude alone wasn't working. I couldn't overachieve at gratitude to feel better.

Worse, I couldn't tell anyone that I was struggling (so I thought). I was the CEO of a company called *Happier*. If you run a company that helps people become happier, you should practice what you preach and be happier yourself, right? How could I reveal that I wasn't? I couldn't break the impenetrable facade of everything's perfect, fine, A-OK, couldn't be better, everything's under control. Not even to my family. That would make me seem like a complete fraud. I couldn't risk it.

Not that they didn't worry about me. Friends, family, colleagues were all concerned. *Don't be ridiculous,* I brushed them aside. *I can do this. I always have.* But I was kidding myself. My *everything is fine* act wasn't working any more. If there was a rock bottom, I was headed right into it. And feeling hopeless was terrifying. This wasn't mere burnout. I was *bottoming out.*

It turned out that my father had given me the key to true happiness twenty-eight years earlier. I was thirteen when we waited in a settlement in Vienna, Austria, to see if we'd make it to America. We lived in a dilapidated apartment building with dozens of other Russian Jewish families trying to make their way to the United States. My parents and I shared a tiny room; they had one of the small beds and I had the other.

One morning when my father came back from the market, where he unloaded crates to make a few dollars, he had an idea.

"C'mon, girls," he said. My mom and I were just waking up. "Let's go see the Vienna Opera House. They have free tours inside and it's supposed to be really beautiful."

"You're crazy!" I told him. "We're living in this disgusting place, we have no money, we have no idea when we'll even get to America if we do, and you want to go sightseeing?"

Sure, I was being a willful teenager, and it's the job of a willful teenager to disagree with their parents. But mostly I couldn't fathom how we could enjoy something while we lived with so much uncertainty and worry. How could we dare to be happy in this moment?

"You're right," my dad told me. "Life sucks right now, absolutely. But we have a choice. We can either sit here and wallow in that, or we can go see something beautiful and enjoy our time here together."

I didn't listen to him. I went along with my parents to see the Vienna Opera House but I made certain that they knew I thought it was a crazy idea. Waiting in line for the free tour, my dad befriended an older gentleman behind us. After the tour, our new friend offered to take us all out for ice cream at the café across the street.

There is a photo of us from that day: Everyone is smiling ear to ear because we're in Vienna, outside the beautiful opera house, having just been treated to *ice cream*! Everyone, that is, but me. A few years after we came to America, I cut my face out of the photo because I couldn't stand my look of stubborn unhappiness.

Back then I couldn't allow myself to enjoy the moment. I was convinced that you don't enjoy little moments when your life sucks. You suffer, you wallow, you *live* your struggle. To find a moment of joy or kindness or beauty when life wasn't okay felt like cheating on reality.

It took me two decades of chasing happiness in all the wrong directions to learn the lesson my dad was trying to teach me way back then: Happiness doesn't arise from making everything in our lives perfect. It comes from embracing life *as it is* and finding small moments of gratitude, joy, kindness, beauty, and human connection *within* it. By truly being present for those moments and being grateful for them, we find the resilience to weather life's storms.

They say the best teachers are those to whom the material they teach didn't come easily. What I'm going to share with you in this book didn't just *not* come easily to me; it went against the very nature of how I thought about life and what happiness truly meant.

Happiness, in my mind, was this idyllic state of contentment that was the opposite of the fear and anxiety I was always feeling after we'd arrived in America. It was a state of amazing that never went away, the BIG HAPPY. But every time I thought I had found it at last—with another achievement, milestone, or accolade—it faded. I had been blowing happiness bubbles that would float beautifully, shimmering in all their iridescent magic, only to burst a short while later.

In fact, it took an ultimatum from one of Happier's investors to stop me in my tracks and start me on one of the most profound (and difficult) journeys of my life. It was a journey that required me to slow down and—this was the most excruciating part—face myself. Not only *face* myself but also accept and *love* myself, as difficult as it still is to say these words. I had to get to a place where I could acknowledge, without falling to self-recriminating pieces, that I was a flawed, imperfect, talented, fun, tightly wound, warm-and-fuzzy human who had a history—and who also had a heart.

Over the course of this book I'll lead you on this journey I took, much to my shock, to find out finally what it really means to be happy. I'll show you what I learned, in the story of what I went through and in the science and practices that have helped me clear a path out of the darkest time in my life. I brought my gratitude practice with me, but I learned that alone, without any other support, gratitude wasn't enough to get me through the very real challenges of life as an entrepreneur, a mom, a wife, a daughter, and a friend, especially since I was already schlepping around a huge bag of heavy feelings from years before that I had never unpacked. I needed to stop judging myself, stop running, and stop piling on insane demands to *just be okay* all the time no matter what.

With the help of an unexpected teacher who became a deeply trusted guide, my patient and loving family and friends, and my own tenacity to find another way, I came up from the dark bottom I had sunk to. No, I didn't become a happy-go-lucky person or start to see everything through a pair of sparkly pink sunglasses. I didn't discover some magic way to find joy in every moment. I *didn't* find the BIG HAPPY that I had been searching for.

I found something way better: I learned to be happier *now*, in this present moment, even if not everything in my life was okay (it never fully is).

Doing this meant taking a huge risk: letting go of striving for perfection. For so many years, perfection seemed as if it would save me from sadness or pain of any kind. I didn't believe that I was good enough as I was, not for myself or for the people around me. We all have our ways of making up for our perceived unworthiness—trying to make a lot of money, to find the perfect love, or even to take care of others without attending to ourselves—and the quest for perfection was mine. It was only when I gave up the possibility of eventually somehow *achieving* my way into a state of uninterrupted happiness by arranging everything in my life, including myself, just so, that I opened up my mind and my heart to embracing all my feelings and experiences, even the "negative" ones. To my surprise, I discovered that if I allowed myself to feel sad, it didn't mean that I would feel sad forever. I also discovered that being compassionate toward myself when I failed, instead of beating myself up, actually encouraged me to try again rather than lulling me into becoming a lazy sloth (that is what I feared) who couldn't deal with reality. Perhaps most surprising was that making the simple yet profound practices of acceptance, gratitude, intentional kindness, knowing my bigger *why*, and self-care part of my daily routine eventually helped me experience the deep sense of contentment that I had been seeking all along.

It still sounds crazy to hear my own words when I stand in front of huge audiences at conferences or corporate events and tell people that the best way to feel happier is to allow themselves to feel unhappy sometimes. We humans aren't meant to feel happy all the time. We live in a culture that tells us, "Be positive! Transform negative into positive emotions! See the glass as half full!" But, in fact, allowing ourselves to feel the full range of emotions, including the ones we see as "negative," offers us a gentler, more inclusive and forgiving path toward happiness and a sense of inner strength and peace. I've come to see that I hadn't failed when I didn't find a way to feel positive emotions all the time; I was doing life exactly right. Deep happiness isn't constrained to only pleasant feelings. It also honors and encompasses our inner strength, sense of meaning, and courageous tenacity to get through the difficult parts of our lives.

This book is organized into two parts. In part 1, I share some of my journey through rock bottom to where I am today. One thing I've learned is that we all want to experience a sense of lasting joy, contentment, and fulfillment, and yet we all struggle to fulfill that desire. Somewhere along the way I began to open up to the Happier community even though it was *very* scary to write honest emails about my struggles and stumbles to a couple hundred thousand strangers. I was admitting that no, I—the CEO of Happier—didn't have a lock on happiness.

But I was blown away by the warmth and encouragement that came back to me in the tens of thousands of emails. It felt like a simultaneous hug from strangers who had become friends overnight. In fact, these emails became my inspiration to write this book and share my journey and lessons learned with you. I realized that we have so much more in common than I had ever imagined. I've been lucky to witness thousands of people transform their lives by implementing the practices

I share with you in this book—people in the Happier community, people who come to my talks and corporate programs, and people who take my online courses. So many people have courageously shared their own journeys with me that I've included their stories throughout to inspire you.

In part 2 we explore the five core practices of acceptance, gratitude, intentional kindness, knowing your bigger *why*, and self-care, and the scientific research that supports each one. I made these practices a core part of my life as I undertook my journey from scary rock bottom toward being genuinely happier. They became my daily anchors. They will help you, too, find more joy in everyday moments, however imperfect they may be. They will also help you hone an essential skill that being truly, genuinely happier requires: the ability to nurture and maintain a healthy emotional immune system, a resilience you can count on to help you through any life storm.

One of the most important shifts I made in my approach to improving my emotional health was to think of happiness as a skill, as something to be *practiced* rather than just *felt*. In each part of the book I include simple exercises to help you strengthen different aspects of your happier skills. Most will only take you a few minutes to complete but their impact can be profound. I encourage you to give them a try. You may discover that some work better than others, and that is totally fine. I suggest that you select a handful—your own daily anchors—that you can do every day and stick to. You can also rotate the practices as different needs come up. The joy is in the doing.

Our to-do lists seem to be ever growing. Whenever I'm tempted to skip doing the practices that I've made part of my routine, I'm reminded of a great Zen saying: "You should meditate for at least ten minutes a day. And if you don't have ten minutes, you should meditate for an hour."

You belong on your to-do list, too, and so does your happiness. It's just too easy to make investing a little time in our emotional health an "extra," something to do after we get all the other "important" stuff done. I've been there, and even after I've seen the amazing and tangible benefits of these practices, I can still get caught in the "I can't take time for myself" negative-talk cycle. If you find yourself there, try this: Think of a person in your life you love very much, someone you really care about. What kind of life do you wish for them?

I think we all would say something similar: we want people we care about to be happy, to find a sense of meaning in their lives, to be with people they love and who love them back. Well, here's the thing: the best way to help people you love be truly happier is to cultivate this practice within yourself. We can't give to others what we don't have ourselves. By investing your energy in improving your emotional health, you're not only doing something awesome for yourself, but you're also giving an amazing gift to people you care about. Research shows that happiness spreads. As you cultivate your happier skills and learn how to find more joy in everyday moments and get through challenging times with more resilience and compassion, you'll be helping your family, your friends, your colleagues, your community do the same. A happier you can be the spark that lights up happiness in so many others.

So let's dive in! I'm grateful you have joined me on this journey.

# part 1

## The Journey to Happier

# 1

# I'll Be Happy When . . .

*We work so hard to get somewhere, to realize a dream, to arrive at some destination, that we often forget that though some satisfaction may be waiting at the end of our endurance and effort, there is great and irreplaceable aliveness in the steps along the way.*

MARK NEPO

In late 2016, I had just finished giving a speech when a woman in a pink leather jacket and a spunky, super-short haircut ran up to me. We were at the New Hampshire Conference for Women, and I was giving the keynote speech about my tumultuous journey to finding genuine happiness and the lessons I learned along way.

"I wanted to make sure I was first in line to talk to you," she smiled. "I'd love to ask you a question about something I'm struggling with at work."

We chatted for a few minutes. I suggested an approach for her work issue, and then with a warm hug we said goodbye. A few days later I got an email from someone named Joy, asking if we had corporate training programs at Happier.

"I was the woman in the pink jacket," she said. Joy turned out to be one of the senior executives at Pure Encapsulations, a company based outside of Boston that makes hypoallergenic, research-based dietary supplements. "I'd love to bring your message about gratitude, kindness, and giving yourself permission to not always be okay to our team here. What I learned from your talk could help a lot of our employees." I told Joy about the Happier at Work training program that I had developed, and several months after we spoke we kicked off the training for all three of her company's offices.

On the first day of the training Joy introduced me to her team. I didn't expect to hear what she had to say.

"After I heard Nataly's talk," she said, nervously looking at her notes, "something changed in me. I had actually taken a personal day because I was feeling so burned-out. I needed to do something just for myself. So I went to this conference in New Hampshire.

"For the past few years I've believed that once our company had its best year ever, once we achieved that amazing milestone, then I would feel really happy. So I just poured all my energy into helping make that happen. And we did. Last year we had our best year ever—by a lot! It was a great accomplishment. But I didn't feel happy. I was exhausted from working nonstop. I was stressed out trying to juggle my work, my travel, and my kids. I wasn't feeling grateful about anything and I wasn't very kind to myself, or, to be honest, to many people around me."

Joy had tears in her eyes. She had worked at this company for twenty years, her entire career after college. For her, the company's success wasn't just a big professional achievement but something deeply personal. She wasn't chasing money, she wasn't after fame or recognition. She wanted the company, the people who worked there, and the products she was passionate about to shine as brightly as they could. She wanted to help more people live healthier lives, and she believed that the supplements her company made could help them do it.

As she spoke, I felt as if I was listening to myself several years earlier. I heard echoes of so much of my own story and feelings.

*How hard both of us had tried,* I thought. I, too, had tears in my eyes.

For most of my life, starting when I was a teenager, I had been invested in the idea that hard work would allow me to accomplish great things, and once I did I would never feel unhappy again. I clung to it as if my life depended on it. As a teenage immigrant in the United States, I was convinced that if only I could learn to speak English without an accent, like a real American, *then* I would be happy. As a thirty-seven-year-old entrepreneur, I was certain that if we could launch Happier and help people improve their lives, then I would, of course, feel happy and nothing else. "I'll be happy when . . ." became my life mantra.

If only I worked hard enough, achieved enough, *then* I would get to this promised land of happiness. Both Joy and I had created this expectation that once our beloved projects or we reached certain milestones *then* we would feel contented forever, and our all-too-real daily human struggles would melt away.

Does this sound familiar to you? When I give talks to companies or at conferences, I ask this question and then pause to look around the room. It's rare to see someone who isn't nodding or who doesn't have that "Oh, I've been there" look on their face. *"I'll be happy when . . ."* is the happiness trap that many of us have fallen into. My circumstances might have been unique, but the conclusion I came to, the idea that I could achieve my way into perfect happiness, is shared by many of us.

On the surface, it makes sense to think that when we achieve something important to us we'll feel happy for a long time. Yet, in reality, it doesn't always work that way; it doesn't allow for the complexity of life, for all the circumstances outside of our control. It doesn't honor the many dimensions of our human experience and our feelings. It's not wrong to hope that something we do will make us happy. But while the goal we're working toward might come true, other things in our lives might go sideways *at the same time*. Or we may quickly get used to our achievement and the euphoria of it will fade. Soon it will just seem ordinary and normal.

The first time I learned this lesson was after I achieved my dream of speaking English without an accent, like a real American.

## I'll Be Happy When . . .

Take out your journal and turn to a fresh page. At the top, write "I'll be happy when . . ." Now list all the things you feel you need to achieve and have in your life to feel happy. Don't judge or edit as you write. Just allow whatever thoughts come to mind to land on your list. These can be really small things or really big life things; there is no right or wrong.

Keep this list in your journal. We'll come back to it later.

## The Dream of Perfect English

When I was thirteen years old, my "I'll be happy when . . ." goal was very specific: I was certain beyond any doubt that I would feel amazing if I could be like Samantha, the main character on the TV show *Who's the Boss?* Sam, played by Alyssa Milano, was a carefree teenager who had a best friend, a pink bedroom, and high-top sneakers with pink shoelaces. I coveted all three with every ounce of my being.

What I wanted the most was to *sound* like Sam, to speak English just as she did. I was certain that when words rolled off my tongue with the same ease as they rolled off hers, my life would change dramatically for the better. After weeks of watching Sam—while stuffing myself with bowl after bowl of Rice Krispies cereal, boxes of which appeared every week in our food donation delivery—I felt a strange sense of relief to be able to define my happiness target so clearly. It became this beautiful image I could escape into, away from whatever I was feeling or whatever was going on.

The best thing about the way Sam spoke English was that everyone understood her and no one made fun of her. This was not the case when I spoke. My English vocabulary didn't amount to much. We had started to learn some English at my school back in Russia, but it was a more bookish, formal English that wasn't especially useful for navigating eighth grade in America. A few months after we arrived in the United States, a boy in my class asked me to go steady, which basically made him a saint since most of my eighth-grade classmates either avoided me or chuckled at me. But I had no idea what he meant. My parents and I tried to look up the words in the dictionary once I got home, but the definitions we found made no sense either. "Move firmly?" It took the poor boy two more tries. He eventually just asked if I would go to the movies with him. *That* I could understand! (I think I said yes.)

I literally didn't know how to express the most basic ideas, such as asking about my class schedule or explaining to the guidance counselor that I didn't have a learning disability but simply didn't know enough English to understand the questions on a test. But worse than my limited vocabulary was my horrible accent. I dreaded saying anything. It usually led to one of two things: utter confusion or smirks and all-out laughter. My eighth-grade teachers favored the former and my classmates the latter.

Several months earlier, with just a few hundred dollars in our pockets, my parents and I had left our home in the former

Soviet Union. I had been shielded from a lot of the difficulties, but even as a child I knew that our life wasn't easy. Often there wasn't enough food or clothes, and everyone, including my parents, spent a lot of time hunting for necessities and standing in line to get them. Lines were a nonnegotiable part of life; there wasn't a line you skipped. You might even get in line without knowing what it was for. You just knew that if there was a line, something very useful and necessary was at the end of it—like toilet paper or milk. One time my dad and grandma took turns standing in line for almost the entire day for boots that my mom and I needed for winter. By the time they got to the end of the line there were no boots in our size, but they bought two pairs anyway and then traded for the right size with people who had also purchased sizes they didn't need.

Being Jewish made our lives even more precarious. The government officially sanctioned persecuting Jews, which meant everything from being barred from certain universities that enforced Jewish quotas to running the risk of being jailed if you were caught following Jewish traditions at home. (We didn't take that risk.) My worst memory of anti-Semitism was not being allowed to travel with my dance group when it went on tour, even when I was a lead in several dances. When applying to come to America as refugees, my parents filled out a thick affidavit with the many, many details of the persecution we had faced.

Our first stop after leaving Russia was Vienna, Austria, where we lived for two weeks in a tiny room in an old building that housed dozens of other Russian Jewish immigrant families. Then we were taken by train to Italy. My parents found us a place to stay in Ladispoli, a small town forty minutes outside of Rome that was already home to thousands of other Russian Jewish refugees. We were all hoping to make it to the United States. My parents and I shared a small apartment with another family whose mom often took over the kitchen to make soup. I had no idea if her food was any good, and none of us knew where she was getting all the ingredients, but the smell made me super hungry. I was hungry all the time, partly because I was a teenager and partly because we didn't have much food. I tried to stay out of the apartment when she was cooking, which was most of the day.

We were allowed to take just two suitcases and $200 per person out of Russia, but my parents had brought some Russian souvenirs after hearing via the refugee grapevine that we could sell them and make a little extra money. Every lira made a difference. Our monthly rent consumed 90 percent of the stipend we received to help us make our journey, leaving us with almost nothing for food. The few extra lira we made selling Russian souvenirs at the makeshift market in the center of Ladispoli helped my mom buy chicken or vegetables with which she made our meals—and each meal had to last. My mom had always been an amazing cook but she became a miracle worker with her determination to feed us on so little.

After two months of waiting, worrying, and battling hunger, we were granted permission to start our lives over in America. Our dream had come true. We got in! A few weeks later, together with several hundred other Russian Jewish refugees, we boarded a chartered plane and flew from Rome to New York. The passengers on the plane erupted into loud applause as we landed. I kissed the ground once we were outside. From there we took another plane to Detroit. We had distant relatives who had immigrated to the United States from Russia a decade earlier, and they lived in Ann Arbor, forty minutes outside Detroit. So we headed there, grateful to know someone would meet us at the airport and help us get around once we arrived.

## Coming to America

Our American dream started off pretty rough. We lived in the projects in Ypsilanti, a small town outside of Detroit, and since we had almost no money, we were set up with welfare, food stamps, and donated furniture. My parents focused on getting jobs, but it was tough because none of us spoke decent English.

I was freaked out. At thirteen, my insides were a soup of hormone-infused adolescent confusion, and immigrating made that soup boil much faster. Everything was unfamiliar, including the simplest things like opening my locker at school—what cruel person came up with the whole once to the right, once to the left, once to the right ordeal? I had no friends, and in a space of three months I had gone from being a top student in my school in Russia to feeling like a mumbling idiot who couldn't figure out the smallest things such as what we had to do for homework. (The teachers would say the assignment too quickly for me to understand.)

That is not to say that there weren't bright spots. Mostly they involved food. When our distant relatives took me to Baskin-Robbins and bought me a banana split, I almost exploded from joy. I couldn't think anything except that *this whole amazing thing is for me!* Domino's Pizza and Lender's Bagels with cream cheese quickly became some of my favorite things to eat—ever. And gum! There was so much bubblegum. When American tourists had visited my school in Russia, we dreamed and schemed of ways to get gum from them. It was the most coveted American treasure. (Twice I had been the lucky recipient, and one of those times I got an entire pack of Bazooka! I cut each piece into quarters and the pack lasted me almost a month. By the end, it was stale but no less wonderful.)

But these food-infused moments of joy were short breaks in the darkness of those early months. Not many of us know who we are at thirteen. Losing the parts of my identity that

I felt defined me, like being smart and doing great at school, left me with a hollowness inside. It quickly filled with worry, anxiety, self-doubt, and this other feeling I've only recently come to understand: fear. I feared everything, from whether we would ever have enough money to move out of the projects, to whether anyone would like me enough to be my friend, to whether I would ever again be able to speak without bracing for the awful confusion or laughter that would come back at me.

I was this petrified for months and months, but I then found Sam on *Who's the Boss?* and she became my hope. I worked my butt off to speak English like she did. Television is a perfect language teacher because you see the way the characters' mouths move when they make certain sounds. I would listen to Sam's character say something and then walk over to the mirror in the hallway and try to imitate the way her mouth moved. I practiced English nonstop, repeating difficult words hundreds of times in a row until I felt I'd improved. (It would take several years of relentless practice and a lot of TV to eliminate my Russian accent, but by the time I got to college one of my classmates asked if I was from New Jersey because I *sounded* like I was from New Jersey. She had no idea that she had paid me the greatest compliment!)

## The Curse of the Moving Baseline

Life definitely got easier and more manageable once I learned to speak English more fluently. And with the help of my parents I also got to imitate a little bit of Sam's American life. For my fifteenth birthday they took me to Payless for high-top sneakers with pink shoelaces—just like Sam's. And for my sixteenth birthday they surprised me by painting my bedroom pink—just like Sam's.

But even though I reached my "I'll be happy when . . ." goal, I didn't feel as happy as I had expected. New things came up all the time—anxiety about making new friends, fear that I wasn't doing well enough. What had seemed like a great way out of my inner turmoil became just a short respite from it.

Reality was a lot less perfect than I'd imagined it to be. The things I'd wanted so much didn't seem as amazing once I had them. My high-top Sam-inspired sneakers turned out to be less awesome as soon as a girl at my school pointed out that they were just an imitation of the cool brand. I didn't realize that you could get the wrong kind of dream sneakers—in Russia we were lucky to get any sneakers, not to mention a choice of different brands. And the day after I got my dream pink bedroom, the bookshelves fell down in a loud crash. Worse, a few of my new friends from school were over and witnessed the whole thing. I was beyond embarrassed, thinking they must know that the bookshelves were cheap. I cursed the damn bookshelves and pink paint job. No matter how hard my parents tried to make me happy, I was too upset to feel grateful.

Still, my internal response was to keep plowing ahead with my "I'll be happy when . . ." mantra. I was convinced that if I worked a little harder and did things the *right* way, then I would be rewarded with the best part of the American dream: being really, really happy, forever. So I just kept racing toward it, working as hard as I could.

I graduated high school third in my class. As I walked from the stage, looking for my parents' proud faces in the auditorium, I was on cloud nine. Against the odds, I had reclaimed my place as a smart, hardworking student. I knew it was a big achievement, as was getting into Wesleyan University and, four years later, graduating at the top of my class not just with high honors but with university honors, an award given to just two graduating seniors. After graduation I was ecstatic to get a job at

McKinsey & Company, the prestigious, it's-harder-to-get-into-than-Harvard consulting firm in New York City. (Of course, I had to explain to my family why this wasn't a total failure because it wasn't law or medical school, which is where I was expected to go after college as a smart Jewish kid. Eventually even my grandparents learned how to explain what I did to their friends and to tell them how prestigious my firm was and that I got to fly business class for work.) Each achievement brought with it much pride and satisfaction, accompanied by the feeling that I *was* doing something meaningful with this gift of being able to build my life in America.

By the time I was in my late twenties, I was a managing director at a venture capital firm in New York City—in an industry with fewer than 6 percent women. I'd also started an educational publishing company together with my husband out of our tiny East Village apartment and landed a book contract from a major publisher to write a book of advice for women. I was running, running, running toward my dream of reaching peace and nirvana. I was doing so much that I became a master of multitasking. I had to—there was so much to do. I'd be rocking my infant daughter, Mia, (because, of course, I had to add being a new mom into the mix) in her bouncy chair with my foot while holding the phone to my ear and analyzing financials on my computer screen.

There is nothing like being an exhausted new mom to push even the most capable overachiever to the brink. I hadn't slept much since Mia had been born and was consumed with worry about doing things right. She cried a ton, didn't sleep for more than a few hours in a row, and was fussy even in the stroller, which, according to her pediatrician, should have been a miracle fix for everything. I was thrown for every imaginable new-mom loop, from dealing with breastfeeding to navigating a thousand conflicting pieces of advice about how to be a good parent. *Put your child on a schedule! Your child is too young for a schedule! Do whatever you can to get your child to sleep! If you rock your child to sleep they will need you to rock them to sleep when they're grown up, married, and have their own kids! Everything changes so don't worry about every choice you make for your child now! Every single choice you make can scar your child for life so don't screw it up!* To make it worse, I felt entirely inadequate in every area of my life—mom, professional, wife, daughter—because I never felt as if I was doing any part of my life really well. I was just running from one to another. If you're a parent, you know what I mean.

One day during my maternity leave, Mia had fallen asleep for her signature twenty-nine-minute nap and I reached for my laptop to dive into my book edits. (The deadline was fast approaching and I didn't think that giving birth to a child was any reason to ask for an extension. That would make me lazy or, worse, incompetent, I thought.) But when I picked up my laptop I just couldn't bring myself to open it. I was just too drained, too exhausted. This was the first time I could remember when I just couldn't push through and keep going.

There was this heavy feeling in my stomach: I wasn't enjoying any of this really great life I had worked so hard to build for us. Deep down I knew it was more than new-mom overwhelm. I'd arrived at a place I'd always dreamed about—great career, loving husband, creative personal projects, adorable new baby. I had it all, and I was proud of what I'd worked so hard to achieve. But I didn't give myself permission to celebrate the many milestones I had reached, to truly swim in the moments of joy and satisfaction they brought. Instead I saw them as stepping-stones to something better I was building for the future. It's as if I was constantly preparing for something else, doing the work to get to a better place, to some final destination where I could truly feel *happy*.

I was going through the now familiar ritual of thinking just how much better things would be when my book came out, when our publishing company was finally sold, when my husband and I got to go on vacation, when we bought our very own apartment instead of renting and Mia could have her own room—*when, when, when.* I kept blowing happiness bubbles, but instead of becoming this one big bubble of lasting contentment, they kept popping. I was burned-out and felt guilty for not feeling happy, having worked so hard to get to where I was. There had to be a different way, but I had no idea what it was.

This turned out to be a gift. Being in this space of not knowing left a tiny opening for an idea to find me. An unexpected idea about what it might take to become truly happy.

*practice* **Five-Minute Joy Break**

Allow yourself to spend five minutes swimming in a little moment of joy. It can be anything at all. Maybe you linger outside to get some fresh air before embarking on your commute to work, sip your favorite latte or tea while flipping through a magazine, or talk to a friend without rushing or checking your phone at the same time. Can you honor these small moments with your entire attention and truly give yourself permission to enjoy them?

# Gratitude to the Rescue

Rejoicing in ordinary things is not sentimental
or trite. It actually takes guts. Each time we drop
our complaints and allow everyday good fortune
to inspire us, we enter the warrior's world.

PEMA CHÖDRÖN

I was an early fan of Zappos, the online shoe company founded by Tony Hsieh. When his book came out, I snapped up a copy. *Delivering Happiness* chronicled the history of Zappos, including Tony's focus on creating a positive company culture to drive successful growth. He filled the appendix with tons of references to scientific research about happiness.

I was intrigued. People studied happiness? Over the next few months I immersed myself in hundreds of studies, articles, and books published on the science behind it. Two things I kept reading about blew my mind.

The first was the idea that happiness isn't a reward we earn for achieving certain things. Rather, happiness is a key ingredient that helps us live a healthier, fuller life and improves our chances of achieving our goals. Here are some of the stats:

- Happier people are healthier and catch fewer colds and flus.

- They have a 50 percent lower risk of having a heart attack or a stroke.

- They live longer.

- They experience less stress and anxiety.

- They have stronger relationships.

- They're more productive. And more creative. And better at customer service. And more liked by their colleagues. They're more successful at work and may even make more money over their lifetimes.

- They sleep longer and better.

I always saw happiness as the ultimate goal, part of the quintessential American dream. So the idea that it could *lead* to so many things I wanted in my life—including being successful—rather than *result* from them, wasn't something I accepted easily. In my mind, happiness was to be earned, a reward given to those who worked really, really hard to achieve it. Even though I hadn't managed to feel it for more than fleeting moments, I was convinced that it simply meant that I hadn't achieved enough yet.

The other theme in my reading was an idea that just seemed ridiculous. The research suggested there were simple things we could all do to significantly increase our emotional well-being without suffering, struggling, or achieving anything. The one habit that came up most often was gratitude, the practice of appreciating the small and big positive moments, experiences, and people in our lives.

When I first started reading about the science behind gratitude and how it benefits our emotional health, I dismissed it completely. I dismissed it even though the research had appeared in well-respected academic journals such as the *Journal of Personality and Social Psychology* and *Harvard Health* publications, and was conducted by professors from top universities, including Martin Seligman, a professor at the University of Pennsylvania and former chair of the American Psychological Association. His book *Flourish* was one of the first I read when I began my research. In it, Seligman describes several studies he conducted with his colleagues on the different practices of gratitude and their results, showing a direct link between gratitude and improved well-being. The practices range from writing down three things you appreciate at the end of the day, to delivering a handwritten thank-you note to someone in your life. The studies were so convincing, the many benefits so vivid, and yet I couldn't get behind *this hokey New Age gratitude thing*. It was definitely *not* going to work for someone as driven and "complex" as me. The whole idea was just too simple, too idealistic, and not *real* enough. Plus, I believed that my suffering was too deeply rooted for anything so seemingly effortless to make a difference. (They say that Russians are good at three things: suffering, making others suffer, and complaining about suffering. It would be funnier if it weren't so true, in my experience.)

I spent about a year reading more books and research studies. The findings were fascinating, even though I remained firmly attached to the belief that they didn't apply to "someone like me."

Here is just a sampling. Did you know that a grateful mindset has been shown to have stronger links to mental health and life satisfaction than most other personality traits, including optimism and hope? In one study, researchers Robert Emmons, a professor at the University of California, Davis, and Michael McCullough, from the University of Miami, randomly assigned one group of participants to keep a weekly list of the things they were grateful for, while other groups wrote down annoyances or neutral events. Ten weeks later, the first group reported having significantly greater life satisfaction than the others.

Gratitude activates the brain stem region that produces dopamine, a neurotransmitter that helps control the brain's reward and pleasure centers. We feel good when we release dopamine—you might have heard it referred to as the "reward" neurotransmitter. Gratitude also stimulates the hypothalamus, which regulates stress, and the ventral tegmental area, which is part of our reward circuitry that produces the sensation of pleasure. (No, I can't really pronounce "ventral tegmental" either, but you don't need to pronounce it to feel the benefits.) Gratitude also increases the production of serotonin, which is responsible for helping regulate our moods. And practicing gratitude turns out to be one of the most effective ways to increase our ability to cope with everyday stresses and traumatic life events. A study published in *Behavior Research and Therapy* in 2006 found that Vietnam War veterans with higher levels of gratitude experienced lower rates of post-traumatic stress disorder.

Grateful people experience an increase in positive emotions and a reduction in stress, and studies show an indisputable direct link between having a grateful mindset and health benefits such as lower blood pressure, less heart disease, better weight control, and healthier blood sugar levels. Research by the American Psychological Association shows that people who practice gratitude have lower levels of inflammation related to heart health.

I could fill dozens of pages with examples of scientific studies that have linked gratitude with increasing our well-being and improving our health. There is literally a mountain of evidence. If there was a magic pill for feeling better, I seemed to have stumbled upon it. But after a year of reading and exploring, I realized that I still hadn't done anything with what I was learning. I wanted to respect the science—my father is a physicist and mathematician, and I grew up with a deep reverence for science—but, ironically, I also wanted to ignore the data. It didn't go well with the story I had told myself about becoming happier. In my version, the only way to get there was through hard work, achievements, and a fair amount of suffering. At best, gratitude felt like cheating, like taking a shortcut.

What finally broke through my stubborn resistance wasn't so much the overwhelming amount of research but sheer desperation. I was completely burned-out. However reluctant I was, I had to try something else, a different approach to feeling happier, more hopeful, less wrapped up in stress and anxiety all the time.

## My Skeptical Gratitude Experiment

I decided that I would give gratitude a try for a month, as an experiment. I was convinced that it would fail and I wouldn't feel any better. Once my suspicions were confirmed—that this practice was too easy and simplistic—I would feel vindicated. I would know that I was better than this cheesy idea.

Every day for a month I committed to writing down three good things about my day. I also tried to have one positive interaction with another person by doing something as simple as pausing and smiling as I said "thank you" to the woman who handed me my coffee at the café rather than mumbling it under my breath as I rushed away.

A few weeks into my experiment, my husband, daughter, and I went to one of our favorite local restaurants. The couple next to us looked new to the place, so I leaned over to suggest a few things on the menu they might try. When the waiter came over we chatted, and then I got up to say hello to the chef, who was busy cooking up a storm in the kitchen.

When I came back to our table, Avi, my husband, gave me a weird look.

"Who *are* you?" he said. "You're talking to strangers, joking with the waiter—?"

"What do you mean, I used to be bitchy or something?" But I already knew what he meant.

"Not at all," he said, smiling. "It's that you're here, with us, and you seem to just be enjoying being here."

My gratitude experiment wasn't failing—quite the opposite. The fabric of my life was becoming richer, not because I changed or added much but simply because I started to pay attention to more of the small moments of joy, awe, kindness, warmth, and connection that were already there. Really tiny moments, like:

- The enthusiasm with which my daughter greeted me at the top of the stairs when I came home from work.

- The way the sun hit the bunch of tulips sitting on our living room table.

- Surprisingly, no traffic on my commute to work.

- A visit from my dad who stopped by with my favorite snack from the Russian store.

- A chilly walk that relieved my headache more than I expected.

- Seeing six feet in funny socks on the coffee table as my husband, daughter, and I settled in for our weekly movie night after an exhausting week.

- The security guard answering my routine "How are you?" with an enthusiastic "Great!"

I hadn't magically become some happy-go-lucky person overnight. These were just some of the tiny moments that had *always* been there. But I had been so used to running right through them, so focused on the big prize at the end, that I'd never noticed them before. My idea of happiness had been idyllic, a pure state. It allowed for no negative emotions or difficult feelings whatsoever. It was such a huge, all-encompassing achievement that I'd assumed tiny moments of joy could never add up to it, so I simply dismissed them as unworthy of my appreciation. Small moments of beauty, warmth, or peace seemed more like distractions than anything meaningful.

But, wow, did it feel good to allow myself to swim in the joy of these little moments! I extended my gratitude experiment from thirty days to several months. In not too long, it became a nonnegotiable part of my daily routine. I talked my friends' ears off about it and about how surprised I was that it could work for someone like me, someone who was so convinced at first that it was a total New Age hoax. If it could work for me, I knew it could work for many others.

So I decided to start a company whose first product would be a beautiful and easy-to-use mobile application that helped people practice gratitude—kind of like a gratitude coach in your pocket. As stressful as it felt at the time to leave my secure, well-paying job at PayPal, I felt compelled to do it. I felt as if I had discovered this amazing secret and I wanted to create a fun, easy way for tons more people to feel the same contentment—and okay, let's just say it, joy—I had been experiencing. Gratitude was easy and it worked. I felt almost evangelical about it.

This is how Happier was born.

## What Are You Grateful For?

We will be exploring the practice of gratitude and suggestions for how to create a gratitude ritual in chapter 7, but I'd love for you to begin right now.

Take out your journal and write down a few things for which you're grateful in this moment. Be as specific as you can. Every tiny one counts. In fact, as we will talk about later, the small things we often forget to appreciate can contribute significantly to feeling happier and more optimistic.

When you finish, pause to consider how you feel. Has anything shifted in your emotions or outlook? Is your experience of this moment, right now, any different than it was before you did your gratitude exercise?

## My Ultimate Proud Achievement

My team and I worked for almost a year to create a mobile app to help people capture and share moments of gratitude. Happier went from just an idea to something that was real and tangible and was now reaching thousands of people. We marked our first release with confetti shooters, cake, and champagne, as we submitted our app to Apple for review (a big moment for new apps). It was tremendous—a surge of feeling accomplished, hopeful, and relieved all wrapped into one big bundle of awesomeness. For many weeks I was bursting with excitement and gratitude.

We didn't have to wait long to know if Happier actually helped people *be* happier. Almost immediately we were flooded with hundreds of emails from users telling us how much they loved the app, and how using it for just a few weeks was helping them feel better, less stressed, more hopeful.

I just wanted to take a moment to thank you for creating this app. As I write this, I am going through one of the most difficult times in my life. By chance, I discovered the Happier app and started seeing these little reminders of everything that is good and beautiful, posted by strangers. Reminders that there is still beauty, goodness, hope, if I look hard enough. So thank you for what you do. It's literally a lifesaver. Love & gratitude.

JOYCE

I'm a medical student and I've wanted to be a doctor all my life. Your app, which I use every day, helps put a smile on my face and quite literally gives me the courage to continue to pursue my dreams. I didn't grow up with a lot of financial or even emotional support. I just had a sense that I could be a really great doctor. Now every day I feel like I am getting closer to that goal. Even though some days are brutally hard, I feel a thousand times better because I have Happier and practice gratitude. And I try to pass on that positivity and hope to every patient I meet. Thank you!!!!!!!!!!!!

NARA

Nothing feels more rewarding and meaningful than to hear that your creation—made from scratch with tons of love, research, and insanely hard work—is making a positive impact on other human beings. As a team, we were so proud.

A few months after we officially launched I got a chance to give a TEDx Talk at TEDx Boston, one of the largest TEDx conferences. I'd given talks at smaller events for entrepreneurs but this was *huge*. It meant that Happier, the company I had been pouring every ounce of myself into, mattered to the world, and I had a chance to share our story. Given that we'd applied past the deadline, it was especially sweet that I still got on the program. My talk was called "How Pancakes Can

Make You Happier and Change the World." In it I shared how noticing and expressing gratitude for the small moments in our lives—such as making silly-looking pancakes to cheer up a dreary winter day—increases our well-being, and how that, in turn, has a positive effect on everyone around us.

When the day came and I was standing on stage in Boston's Seaport World Trade Center auditorium, I wore a bright orange dress—orange is the official Happier color—and more makeup than seemed healthy. My heart was jumping out of my chest but I didn't feel nervous; I was a ball of hyper energy ready to be released once I started to speak. This felt like my ultimate proud achievement because I finally thought, after more than two decades of hard work, that what we were doing at Happier and our mission to help millions of people live more fulfilling lives was important and valuable enough to make the struggles my family had gone through as refugees worth it.

Toward the end of the talk I asked the audience to share their own moments of gratitude. We'd given out name tags that had extra space to write on. As everyone was writing with their orange markers, I took a deep breath. I was going to lead the way by sharing my own happy moment.

"Being able to stand here and share my story and the story of Happier and our community with you is a huge achievement, and I'm really grateful for it," I said. "But that's not my happy moment. My happy moment is to be able to share this experience with my parents, who are my ultimate heroes for bringing me here."

I tried to keep it together, but it was hopeless. Through the bright lights I saw my parents sitting in the second row to my right, their faces glowing with pride and joy. My dad's face was covered with tears while my mom cried on the inside, as she does. I couldn't hold back my own tears. The audience erupted into applause as my parents' faces were projected on the big screen behind me. All I wanted was to stop time so the three of us could just be there together in this amazing bubble of pure happiness for as long as possible.

"We made it!" I wanted to scream. I stifled my desire to run and hug them. "We made it!" I felt proud, vindicated, victorious, accomplished. My parents decided to leave the former Soviet Union for many reasons—crumbling economy, restrictions on everything, from which books we could read to where we could travel, and the ever-present disparity between the difficult reality of our lives and the everything-is-perfect party line. They also wanted to escape the constant persecution we faced as Jews. But the main reason they left was to try to give me a chance at a better, brighter, freer future. It felt incredible to know that I was doing right by them. I hadn't wasted that chance. It was one of the greatest moments of my life.

## Chasing Perfect Happiness

With the successful launch of Happier I had achieved my biggest *"I'll be happy when . . ."* moment. I'd finished the sentence: "I'll be happy when I do something important and meaningful that truly honors my gift of being able to grow up in America." For a time, I *was* really, really happy. This experience felt similar to many of my previous achievements—like a bubble of happiness. And just like before, I hoped that the burst of positive emotions I was feeling would help me finally escape from the insecurity, self doubt, and anxiety that had become all too familiar since we began our refugee journey.

But they didn't. After a while the bubble of happiness popped, revealing many stresses, fears, and worries, some of which had been there well before Happier and some that came with the challenges of building a start-up from the ground up.

My gratitude practice continued to help me notice and appreciate many good moments in my days, but all the difficult feelings were still there.

What I discovered, once again, was that our achievements *do* make us happy and proud, but all the other emotions we collect on the way there, including the really difficult ones, aren't simply replaced with our joy and excitement. Maybe you think, *I'll be happy when I make more money; when I find my soul mate; when the weather is nicer; when we move to a better house; when my baby stops crying and sleeps through the night; when I get a promotion* or *when I get a better job; when I lose weight and get into better shape.* We've all had thoughts similar to these at one point or another. And I'm sure you *will* feel great when you reach your "I'll be happy when . . ." goal. But as Joy—the woman I introduced you to in chapter 1—and I learned, you'll also experience many other feelings. This one achievement won't miraculously make everything else in your life perfect. (But, oh, how we wish.)

Of course there's nothing wrong with working hard to achieve something or reach a milestone. As we'll talk about in chapter 9, when what we do brings us a sense of meaning, it contributes to our sense of well-being and happiness. But we can't use achievements to cover up feelings we don't want to feel or to shield ourselves from challenging moments that we inevitably encounter in the course of our lives. That only works for a very short time, then the happiness bubble pops, the bandage falls off, and we're left not only with the same challenges and difficult feelings we might have tried to run away from but also a sense of disappointment for having failed to find perfect and lasting happiness. But unless someone shows you the way, or life itself intervenes, you can keep chasing those happiness bubbles for a very long time.

I did.

It turned out that my major milestone with launching Happier wasn't the end of my fear, stress, and anxiety. In fact, it was the beginning of a heart-wrenching deep dive into a pile of pain that I had ignored for years and that I had been hoping to escape by achieving my way into a sense of peace and endless bliss by way of my "I'll be happy when . . ." mantra.

## 3

# The Breaking Point

*Tell your heart that the fear of suffering
is worse than the suffering itself.*
PAULO COELHO

Happier wasn't my first start-up, but it was the one with the highest personal and professional stakes. Let me be more honest about this: *Happier mattered to me in a way no other company I'd launched or worked at ever had.* It was literally born out of my life story, and this was our main marketing narrative—how I went from being a refugee to the United States to starting a company to help people be happier. As CEO, my signature was on everything from investor agreements to employee letters. I was responsible for our team, for figuring out which direction to lead us, for the satisfaction of tens of thousands of people who would come to use Happier. I felt intense pressure to make Happier a success.

Some of the stress I felt came from the real challenges of getting the company off the ground. Our team quickly grew, almost tripling in size, and at times some of the interpersonal dynamics didn't work. Features we thought users would love—they didn't. We were constantly trying out new things and didn't always take enough time to learn why they did or didn't work. Plus, we needed to raise more money to keep our doors open and to keep developing the app. We didn't have a lot of data yet, so this wasn't going to be easy.

As the months rushed past after our launch, my thoughts gripped me tighter and tighter. I was afraid of failing, of screwing up, of running out of money, of the team not being satisfied, of not being a competent leader. When you move into fear, everything in your world narrows, even your field of vision as your entire body focuses its energy to fight whatever it is you're afraid of. My world narrowed and I didn't think about much else. The voice in my head was on a constant loop of a "what if" narrative—*What if this doesn't work? What if the whole gratitude thing doesn't work in an app? What if we run out of money? What if I have to lay off the team? What if . . . ?* Fear began to color every interaction and experience.

I know I'm not the first entrepreneur to feel this way. My friend Chetan completely burned-out getting his start-up off the ground while also trying to keep up with his graduate classes at MIT and Harvard. As a fellow overachiever, he was getting a double degree. He showed all the physical signs of burnout: weight gain, chronic tiredness, bags under his eyes. Being constantly distracted by work strained his relationship with his family.

"The primary thing I remember is a vicious cycle of self-doubt and poor performance," Chetan told me. "Negative thoughts were constantly cycling through my brain: *This won't work. Focus on something you're better at. You're not made to be an entrepreneur!* They actually prevented me from excelling. Then when my performance on those tasks didn't live up to my expectations, the negative chatter would get louder."

When you create something you care about, you worry about not being able to pull it off. Happier was my boldest attempt yet to do something valuable and important with my life. Entrepreneur friends tell me similar stories: fear and uncertainty come with the job. But in my mind, if Happier didn't work, I was a total failure as an entrepreneur *and* as a human being. I'd blended my identity as Nataly with my company, Happier. I tied up my self-worth with the company's success. How could I go on if I failed?

# Breaking Fear
# into Parts

This is a practice I wish I had done when I was overcome by my fear of failing because it would have helped me avoid becoming completely paralyzed by it. We all have things we fear. Maybe you're thinking about switching jobs and worry about giving up something secure for a riskier path. Or perhaps you fear having a difficult conversation with someone important to you.

Bring to mind something you really want, but you're afraid to do. Then open your journal and complete this sentence: "I'm afraid of . . ."

When you have a clear idea what you're afraid of, break up your fear into smaller parts. Here are some questions to guide you:

**What specifically are you afraid of?** For example, if your fear is that you won't do as well as you want on an upcoming presentation at work, are you afraid of how your colleagues will see you, how your boss will critique you, how vulnerable you'll feel? Be as specific as you can.

**What will happen if this fear comes true?** Consider the worst-case scenario for a second and write about how you might feel and what would change in your life. Do you think you could get through it, and what are some things that would help you do that?

**Is your fear helpful?** Some parts of fear can be helpful if they prompt you to learn something about how you feel or what you might need to do. No need to be afraid of your fear! Other parts might be getting in your way and wasting your energy.

I don't believe in being fearless. If you're a human being, you'll feel fear at some points in your life. It's completely normal. But this exercise can help you break up your fear into more manageable parts and avoid treating it as a paralyzing obstacle.

## Keeping Secrets, Saving Face

If you think I told anyone about the fear and doubt I felt, you'd be wrong. My husband and a few close friends knew, but not fully. I told no one else.

I'd never met a leader who shared their doubts or anxieties as they were experiencing them. When you hear entrepreneurs or leaders talk about being uncertain about their company's future, it's usually in retrospect, *after* they've figured out what they're doing and where they're going. So like most other entrepreneurs, I tried my best to act like a confident, need-no-sleep superhuman and to hide the increasingly paralyzing fear that I felt. I thought to share it would make me weak, and I did not want anyone to think I wasn't up to the job.

But my friends, family, and colleagues weren't stupid; they knew something wasn't right. During one of our weekly team meetings, we had a big debate about making a significant change in the way our users experienced courses in the Happier app. Everyone had a strong opinion and the discussion went on for more than an hour.

"Nataly?" one of our team members asked, looking at me strangely. I hadn't said a word. I *never* had nothing to say. I *always* had opinions. In fact, the problem usually was that my opinions were too strong. But I simply couldn't find the energy to come up with anything intelligent. I couldn't focus. My mind was caught in a fear-and-doubt spiral.

More people started to ask frequently if I was okay. "Oh, I'm just stressed. You know, the usual." I brushed it off, trying to project an everything-is-okay, totally-got-this vibe. I've always been convincing when it comes to being upbeat. And I was the CEO of a company called *Happier*. How could I reveal that I wasn't happy—at all—and that I couldn't practice what I preached? Everyone would think I was a total fraud if they knew just how stressed, sad, and anxious I felt. *Was* I a total fraud, peddling this idea of gratitude as the path to happiness while being increasingly unable to feel even small moments of joy in my own life? What would our Happier users think if they found out how I truly felt?

In fact, gratitude was one of the ways in which I tried to cope. The more anxious and worried I felt, the more gratitude I practiced. I became a gratitude overachiever, some days sharing more than ten happy moments in the Happier app. They were all real and I treasured them, but I increasingly shared them out of desperation. Maybe if I found enough good moments, *then* I wouldn't feel like such a mess.

But you can't replace stress with gratitude. You can't remove anxiety with joy. You can't simply ignore the pile of painful feelings growing inside of you and cover it with gratitude like a bandage. It doesn't work that way. As hard as I tried to keep it together, to move forward, to put on my *can-do!* face every day, I was slowly losing my ability to function.

## The Vicious Cycle of Self-Doubt

My inability to carry on with my "everything is fine!" act spilled from work to home, although I didn't fully grasp it at the time. I was becoming a shell of myself. I was fixated on the endless stress and worry about the company while moving at a frantic pace to solve problems. I zoomed past those closest to me, unable to fully connect with them.

Avi wasn't new to the intensity of the ups and downs I experienced while running a start-up. We had been together for fifteen years, so he'd seen a lot. Naively I believed that he was so laid back that he could handle it when I unleashed my waves of stress, panic, and fear on him. That was a farce. Avi, who had always been my rock, my comfort, was running out of his usual kind patience. The more he pulled back, the more I resented losing the support and care I'd come to rely on. I unleashed more and more of my fear and stress on him, hoping to feel that comfort once more. When I didn't, I got more resentful. Eventually, we just stopped talking.

My marriage turned into a series of cold transactional exchanges about who got home when, who needed to pick up what, with interludes of snippy comments. There wasn't one part of me available to consider doing anything about it. It's not that I stopped loving my husband. It was more like someone had locked away any good, loving feelings in a safe and threw away the combination.

My daughter, who was nine at the time, began to look at me with deep worry in her beautiful big eyes. She hesitated to ask me anything, from how my day was to whether she could go on a playdate with a friend. She seemed to want to avoid poking through my thin protective layer at all costs. She'd already seen enough of my stress spilling out. I'd yell at the top of my lungs when she dropped something on the kitchen floor—then I'd cry uncontrollably from the guilt of yelling at her. When we were a few minutes late to her piano lesson, I'd curse and honk at every car that drove slower than I wanted to, completely losing it.

Sucking as a mom was intensely painful. Even recalling this now makes my heart twitch. The voice in my head shifted from the loop of terrible "what ifs . . . ?" to scenarios of total failure: *You're obviously no good as an entrepreneur! And you're being a terrible mom and a wife. You're just a failure, that's all! And you have failed at your American dream. What a waste!*

The self-doubt was terrible but it wasn't new. What made it so much worse was that it wasn't just related to Happier. It was tied to who I was as a human being. I'd felt it, along with feelings of anxiety and fear of failure, for a very long time. I had chased achievements to try to escape these feelings, to blow enough happiness bubbles so that the good emotions would leave no space for anything negative. But the pile had only grown, and now I couldn't keep carrying it around anymore. All these feelings started to spill out. I didn't just have them, I became them.

Soon I reached a point I never, ever thought I would. I was Nataly. I was tough, resilient—beyond resilient. A super overachiever. But I couldn't fake it anymore, not even me. I reached a breaking point.

I was going through the motions of my life but I wasn't really there. I sat with my team during key discussions, not saying a word. I didn't feel like I was in the room with them. Then I'd stay late at the office without knowing what I was trying to accomplish. I often found myself sitting in my car in the parking garage after work, not sure if I was coming in to work or going home.

Normally I have *no* trouble getting things done. Even in the most stressful situations I can plow through bajillions of tasks. I used to feel smug when reading articles about people having trouble being productive. Now I couldn't complete even the simplest things on my to-do list.

I went to business meetings over breakfast and lunch only to suddenly realize that the person I was meeting had already left but I was still just sitting there, with no idea what I was doing in the restaurant or what I was supposed to do. Clearly, I needed to do *something* because the waiter was almost screaming at me, "Ma'am, are you okay?"

Once on a business trip to San Francisco, I arrived unable to remember what it was all about. One of the things my family always talks about is my foolproof memory. (My husband jokes that he wishes he had that magic memory-eraser pen like the guys in *Men in Black* so that I wouldn't remember all his little mess-ups for years after they happened, like the time he drilled a hole through our kitchen wall straight into the living room while hanging up a painting.) But now I had to search through my emails to remind myself what I was doing in the Bay Area.

At home I'd find myself frozen in the middle of playing Connect 4 with my daughter, zoned out and drifting far away from reality. *You're a failure and won't ever do anything right!* was looping in my mind. Mia would look at me with confusion, but also with patience, as if she was getting used to this new version of mom.

A breaking point feels exactly like it sounds, like every single thing inside you and in your life is broken: your work, your family, your basic life functions. I either ate too much or nothing at all. I drank too much wine. I stopped doing anything I enjoyed, like going to museums or watching movies, two of my favorite things. I slept in short increments of a couple hours here and there. I tried to avoid any unnecessary interactions with other people, including my parents, friends, and the team in the office. A single day seemed to contain years. It was dark, like a light inside of me had been extinguished. All I could feel was dread.

## This Isn't Happening

"Listen, you're not okay." I was having lunch outside on a chilly October day with Mike, an investor in Happier and a trusted friend.

"What do you mean?" I tried to wave him off.

He wouldn't let it go. "You're not okay. You need to focus on yourself. Right now, nothing else matters."

In my gut I knew he was right. More and more, my team, friends, and family had been urging me to take a break, to catch my breath, to take care of myself. I rushed away from their concerned looks and questions. I changed topics, shifted conversations. I kept my wall up. Even Avi had reached across the cold distance between us and asked me to consider shutting down the company. It wasn't that he didn't want Happier to survive, but rather he was worried that *I* wouldn't survive.

I dismissed his idea as absurd. Happier was everything to me. I *was* Happier.

But my wall wasn't strong enough to keep Mike out. He cared about Happier and our success, but he also cared about me as a person. If Mike was telling me that I needed to focus on me rather than the company, I must be in really bad shape. (A year later I found out that it was my husband who had called him to try to get through to me.)

I also knew that Mike had gone through his own personal hell. Since we'd met, his marriage had ended and he'd gone through a difficult divorce. At the same time, he had been starting his own venture fund, essentially building a company from scratch and enduring all the stresses and worries that come with that. We had spent many hours talking about what he was going through, and I had rushed to see him many times when he really needed a friendly ear. Having witnessed his vulnerability created a tiny space for my own.

That and the fact that Mike gave me an ultimatum.

"You're going to focus on yourself," he said firmly. "And you're going to go see this woman—her name is Janet. Until then, I'm not going to talk to you about Happier."

Oh.

It may have been Mike telling me to get help, but there was one thing I certainly was *not* doing: seeing a therapist. First of all, *we* don't do that. By "we" I mean Russian Jewish immigrants who are trained to bear whatever pain there is, to put it away in a steel box, lock it, and keep moving forward. Sit around and talk about our problems, feelings, and childhoods? No, thank you. Therapy had always seemed like a uniquely weird American idea. So useless! So self-indulgent!

Second of all, *I* didn't do that. And by "I" I mean Nataly Kogan, who had everything together: a successful career, a beautiful family in a beautiful house in a beautiful neighborhood with a cute Mini Cooper in the garage, and a large collection of big, funky rings. In my mind, going to "see someone" was like waving a huge white flag of defeat above my head. It was the ultimate sign of weakness. It would show that I'd failed at being the fighter-warrior who can do life on her own.

"Listen," I tried to match Mike's firmness, "I don't really do therapy."

"I don't care." He looked me in the eye. "But also she isn't a therapist. I'm texting you her number."

I was shocked. As he got up to leave, he added, "Go see her and then I'll talk to you about business again."

As I sat there, stunned, my mind went crazy. My first thought was *I'm not doing this. No way.* Then, *I just need to get some sleep and get my thoughts organized, then I'll be better. He'll see.* Then, *I'm just not cut out to run a company. I'll sell Happier and then I'll feel better.* Then, *I want to run away somewhere, do my own version of* Eat, Pray, Love, *take a break from myself, close my eyes, and sleep for a really long time, like forever.*

As I got up and walked away from our lunch, I tried and tried to shut down these swirling thoughts. I was Nataly. I could change direction, compartmentalize, bounce back. But the thoughts persisted; they had been there for all the months and years of creating Happier—and long before that. They weren't going away. In my gut I knew I needed Janet or someone else. Anyone. I needed help, desperately. But I dreaded calling her. I put it off. It took a few more weeks to "think about it." A few more weeks of dysfunction and dread.

"Mike told me I should come see you." I was giving in and scheduling an appointment. "I don't really know if this is for me, but . . ."

"It's okay," the voice on the other end of the line was soft and comforting, free of expectations. "I understand."

When I opened the door to Janet's office for the very first time, I felt like I was stepping off a cliff.

## My Unlikely Guide through the Storm

Mike was right; Janet wasn't a therapist. I didn't know what she was, but eventually she became my teacher and my spiritual guide.

Luckily, she didn't say the word *spiritual* when we met. I was allergic to the word because "people like me" didn't do "stuff like that." There had never been a spiritual or religious thread in my life. We are Jewish, but it's a cultural identity rather than a religious one. All forms of religion were illegal for most of my life in Russia, but Jews in particular weren't allowed to participate in any customs or ceremonies. When we'd been invited to celebrate Jewish holidays in America shortly after we immigrated, we had no clue what we were doing.

But it was more than that. Somewhere along the way I'd adopted the view that any religion or spirituality was a crutch. Only those who couldn't hack "real" life used it. I thought of spirituality or religion in the same way as whenever anyone talked about "circumstances beyond our control"—rich with excuses that people latched onto to make life easier. And I didn't *do* easy. I was a fighter-warrior who knew the "real" truth in life: anything worthwhile was to be found through fighting, struggling, and suffering. (If I'm being really honest, I had no clue about what spirituality even meant, but this didn't weaken my conviction about it.)

But here I was, sitting in a big plush armchair in front of this woman with short gray hair, her hands resting in her lap. Our first meeting had a lot of silence in it. Janet didn't prod me with many questions and I didn't really know what to say. She asked me how I knew Mike and I launched into telling her about Happier, our vision, why it mattered so much, how difficult it was, and how we needed to raise money. It was as if I was talking to a potential investor or someone I needed to impress. Janet nodded patiently as I talked. I'm sure it didn't take her long to figure out that it was easier for me to talk about the company than about how I felt.

"I guess I'm really exhausted." I thought it was safe enough for a CEO of a start-up to admit to *that* without seeming weak.

"Well, of course you are," she said. "You've got so much on your shoulders, so many people you're taking care of, so much pressure. Of course you're exhausted."

Janet didn't try to change what I said or how I felt, or try to fix or question it. She was so generous that I immediately wanted to cry. And run to hug her. And never leave her little office ever for the rest of my life. But, of course, I did none of that. Instead I used a crazy amount of willpower to look nonchalant and strong, unmoved. But I was overcome with a strange and unfamiliar feeling. What *was* it? I loved it.

It felt safe.

It felt like relief.

It felt like coming home.

It was the feeling of being unconditionally accepted.

I left Janet's office that day knowing I had experienced something profound. Talking with her gave me a tiny break from feeling as if I was fighting with every part of myself and my life.

Yet I didn't know what to do with it. If I kept going to Janet, would I become some lazy cop-out who never did anything meaningful again? Did I have to exchange my ambitions and goals for a life of sitting in a comfy plush chair doing nothing?

## No Way Back

I didn't tell anyone that I went to see Janet—except Mike, so that he knew I'd taken his advice. After a few weeks, I told Avi.

"She's this woman Mike knows," I said without giving any details about who she was or what we talked about. The funny thing is that *I* didn't really know who she was or what exactly we talked about. I just knew that when I was with her I didn't have to pretend or to run so fast. I could just *be*. And that felt amazing.

I kept going back. Janet let me go on with my defeatist self-talk for as long as I wanted—how I was weak, an imposter, and a failure.

"You're not a failure. It's that you've tried to numb any pain you feel with all your accomplishments," Janet would say after some time. "But that has stopped working for you. It's the way of the ego, not of your higher self."

No part of me was ready for words such as *higher self*.

"I certainly feel like failure! I can't function in this life that I worked so hard to build," I argued, fighting back tears. "It's like I can't handle my real life so I'm looking to escape from reality."

"You *are* looking for another way," she said, finally. "It's not an escape from reality. It's a way to live your life being guided less by your ego that keeps convincing you that you need to do more, more, and more to earn your own love and love of other people in your life.

"You need to learn to love yourself and be kind to yourself," she said. Janet was calmly shattering everything I had ever understood. "Just for who you are, exactly how you are. Your higher self knows you don't need to do a single thing. You don't need to *earn* love."

How was it possible to just like myself for who I was when I had grown up with the fundamental understanding that life is all about improving myself, pushing myself to learn and do more and do it better? How could I even consider something in me like a *higher self* that was somehow more true to me than my so-called ego, which had driven me feverishly to chase everything I had achieved so spectacularly?

On days when I had profound experiences like this with Janet, the voice in my head went into overdrive to make sure I didn't take them too seriously. *This is just some escapist spiritual mumbo jumbo. It's for the weak. You're just being weak if you listen to it! You're here because you've failed at life!*

There is a saying that suffering is the sandpaper necessary to bring about happiness. There is a point where the pain of that rough surface on our vulnerable selves makes it urgent that we find relief. Perhaps I'd been sandpapering myself long enough that I finally had no choice: I had to open up. I'd been constantly chasing achievements, pushing aside old pain, fear, and sadness that I had no idea how to process, and then working harder and harder every day to pretend that everything was okay. For me, pain and suffering were what I knew how to listen to. *Did I really want to continue to live this way?*

## Your
## Safe Place

Take a few moments to think and write about where or when you feel accepted and safe. It could be with a person, someone with whom you feel comfortable being yourself just as you are, without having to put on an act. Or perhaps it's a special location, such as your favorite spot in nature. Maybe you feel as if you're truly home when you're doing an activity, such as yoga or writing.

It's important to remind ourselves about the people, places, or things that help us experience that magical feeling of being okay just as we are. Even if we can't always access them, knowing that they're there for us can be comforting, especially when we're going through small or big life storms.

# 4

# It's Okay to Be Not Okay

What a caterpillar calls
the end of the world
we call a butterfly.
ECKHART TOLLE

I was in a storm and the only way out was through it.

"It will get better," Janet told me. "When you stop serving your ego, the universe will help you. But for a while it will be very hard."

She wasn't kidding. It was hard. Hard to acknowledge that "all that immigration stuff" wasn't some story that was behind me. Hard to recognize that it was at the very core of who I was and the pain that I carried. Hard to stay with my feelings for any length of time before the voice in my head started to scream about how pathetic I was.

To give me courage, I printed out a passage from one of my favorite authors, Haruki Murakami: "And once the storm is over, you won't remember how you made it through, how you managed to survive. You won't even be sure whether the storm is really over. But one thing is certain. When you come out of the storm, you won't be the same person who walked in. That's what this storm's all about."

I carried his words everywhere as if they were proof that I would survive.

One day Janet remarked, "Your English is amazing—you have no accent at all. Hard to believe you didn't really start speaking English until you were thirteen."

"It's one of my proudest achievements," I replied. I told Janet the story of Sam on *Who's the Boss?* with her great American life, pink bedroom, and high-top sneakers with pink shoelaces. I told her about my family's trip to Payless when I was fifteen, the pink paint job in my bedroom when I was sixteen, and how the bookshelves had collapsed in front of my teenage friends to my utter mortification.

Over time I went deeper, opening up about things I hadn't realized were even a big deal. I'd put my entire refugee experience in a box, with all of its pain and confusion, and tried my hardest to make it something that lived only in my past. But it turned out that all these things were a *huge* deal. They were as much a part of me now as they were then, perhaps even more because I'd bottled them up for so long.

One day I told Janet about one of my most painful memories from the time when we were trying to make our way to America. Before leaving Russia my parents had sent some food ahead, knowing that we wouldn't have money to buy much in the refugee settlement. The tricky part, other than finding enough nonperishable food that didn't taste horrible, was where to send it. We didn't know where we would be living or exactly when we would get there. So my parents, like many others who were fleeing, sent boxes of canned vegetables and fish to a post office in Rome and hoped for the best.

Miraculously, when we got to Italy one of the boxes was there. One very hot July day, my father and I traveled the hour into the city to find the post office. My dad carried the heavy box back to the train station, shifting it from one shoulder to the other every few minutes. It was extremely humid and the streets were crowded. I remember seeing sweat pouring from my dad's forehead and glistening on his thick beard. We had brought one small bottle of water with us, but he drank from it just once to make sure that I would have enough. I wanted to do something to help, but what could I do? The box was too heavy for me to carry and my dad wouldn't take another sip of water even when I offered it to him. The feeling of not being able to help the people you love is awful. I hated it.

I hadn't realized that I was going to tell Janet this story, but the moment I did everything shifted. I mean a huge, seismic kind of shift. A big light went on: I'd grown up believing that love and suffering were inseparable. My dad's strength and his sacrifice that day in Rome was the essence of love. To truly love someone, I believed, you had to suffer for them. You had to not take more than a sip of water on a superhot day so the other person had more to drink. Or you had to slave over dinner, like my grandmother in Russia had done so often, grinding herself to the brink of collapse. You had to keep your confusion, pain, and fear inside, as I tried to do, so you wouldn't add to the worry your family members already had on their plates.

## Hiding Suffering Behind Love

When people ask me what was the hardest thing about immigrating to America, two things compete for first place: not knowing English and not being able to rely on my parents to guide me through our new life. You can't do a thing when you don't know the basics of a language. Feeling idiotic and confused was tough for all of us. For a time, we were completely lost, and my parents were as lost as I was.

In America our roles of parent and child sometimes reversed. Since I learned English much faster than they did, I often became my parents' guide, the translator, the one who figured things out. I helped my parents open bank accounts and ask for things at the pharmacy. While teenagers often want to be their parents' equals, it's surreal when it actually happens. Many teenage immigrants say the same thing: when you become the guide, you feel as if you lose your protection.

One day, a few months after we arrived, my mom made me a hot dog sandwich for lunch, using dark rye bread, somewhat like the dark bread we ate in Russia. When I unwrapped the sandwich in the school cafeteria, one of the kids at my table looked over curiously. Then he chuckled and called over a few of his friends.

"Don't you know what a hot dog bun is?" one of them asked.

"No." I regretted unwrapping my sandwich. I regretted coming to America. I regretted being born.

Soon, dozens of kids had formed a roaring circle of laughter around my lunch table. I guess it really was funny to see such a weird version of a hot dog sandwich. It took all my determination not to cry.

But what made me feel that much worse was learning that my dad had had a similar experience at work that day. My mom had made him the same approximation of an American sandwich and his colleagues had also had a nice laugh at his expense. As he told us about it, he brushed it away with a smile. But I was angry at his colleagues: no one made fun of my brilliant father! I was angry at my classmates for humiliating me, but more than that, I was angry that my dad and I were being made fun of for the very same thing. Your parents should protect and guide you. Mine could do neither and that was lonely and scary.

I tried to keep my anxiety inside as much as I could. Mostly I didn't want to burden my parents with my "stuff" because they had enough to worry about as they began to build our new lives from scratch. If I pretended that things were okay, it would make life easier for them—that is, until I could make everything okay for us. I was going to be the first real American in our family, and I'd pass along all those benefits and privileges just as soon as I could.

Don't get me wrong. I wasn't some dream child—far from it. Like other teenagers—but with a certain Russian intensity and flair for drama—my confusion and turmoil sometimes boiled over. I had bouts of screaming, fighting, and door slamming. I went on a short-lived hunger strike and once ran out of the house and threw myself down on the sidewalk. (My dad had to come pick me up.) My parents tried to get me to talk to them. I still remember the pained worry in my mom's beautiful eyes as she sat on the edge of my bed, asking me to tell her what was wrong, but I refused.

My family had always been incredibly loving, but we didn't talk about difficult emotions much. Partly this was out of love: we wanted to protect each other from being burdened with our own suffering. We didn't admit to things for years, and sometimes not at all. The first time my father mentioned that he was scared when we lived in refugee settlements was just a few years ago when we were planning our twenty-fifth anniversary party of our arrival in America. And even then he made a joke about it.

I had adopted the belief that the way to deal with something bad was to move past it. You fall down, you get up and keep going. This fighter spirit is one I cherish. It helped us overcome the obstacles we faced to build a new life in America, and it's my trusted ally for getting through challenges even now. But just because you fight through your difficult feelings doesn't mean you don't feel them or that they go away. Mine had piled up into a big dark heap, one that I was now, for the first time, starting to experience rather than run from.

## What Do You Google to Heal Your Soul?

A few months after I met Janet I began to attempt to be with the pain that I'd tried to cover up with achievements, to feel it and try to heal it.

This idea was scary for three reasons:

- It felt very much like the cop-out of someone who couldn't handle "real" life.

- It meant that I had to shift my priorities from work and family to myself, something I'd never done in my life. Also, doing this only reinforced point one.

- I didn't feel that I deserved to do it, and the guilt of doing something I didn't feel I had earned was brutal.

Even as I fought this idea (or as my ego fought this idea), I knew it was the only way to begin to climb out of this darkness that had consumed me for the past year and endangered everything that was dear to me, including my family and my company.

So how do you heal your soul?

At first I thought, *I'll Google it.* It sounds crazy to me now. Why would Google know but not Janet? The truth is, Janet rarely told me what to do. She created a space in which I could stop trying so hard and then, inevitably, ideas about what I wanted to do came to me. So after a few months inching toward concepts I had naturally rejected up to that point—such as soul or spirituality—I came home and Googled "Top books about spirituality."

One of the books that came up was *Be Here Now* by Ram Dass. It seemed totally weird and "woo-woo." I kept thinking, *I've definitely lost it!* The book was thick, square, and printed on newsprint with hand drawings and handwritten passages such as, "It's only when caterpillarness is done that one becomes a butterfly. That again is part of this paradox. You cannot rip away caterpillarness. The whole trip occurs in an unfolding process of which we have no control."

*Whaaat?*

But I was impressed by Ram Dass's bio. He was no lightweight hippie. In fact, he had been Richard Alpert, a successful psychology professor at Harvard, with many degrees from top universities including a master's from Wesleyan, my alma mater. He was the son of very successful Jewish parents—his father had been one of the founders of Brandeis University. When academics failed to give him a deep enough understanding of the meaning of life, he experimented, as many people did in the 1970s, with psychedelics. Then he went to India where he studied for ten years with a guru. When he returned to the United States as Ram Dass, he became a prominent spiritual leader. Even though he had a major stroke in the late 1990s, he still teaches today.

Ram Dass came from a place I could understand. That helped me pause my judgment long enough to trust his words. If he quit all that to devote his life to spiritual practice and meditation, surely I could spend an hour a day on healing my soul, as I began to call it.

Toward the end of *Be Here Now* there is a short manual for how to start on a yogic or spiritual path, including suggestions for yoga postures, breathing practices, and meditation. I had been going to yoga classes for a few years, but mostly to get a physical reset and a break from the hectic tempo of my daily life. My experience with meditation was limited to the few minutes when our yoga teachers would ask us to sit and focus on our breathing. And it was never very successful. My mind would usually go into a spiral of thoughts ranging from obsessing about my to-do list to judging myself for fidgeting. But it seemed as if every day new research proclaimed the benefits of meditation, so I decided to give it a try.

## My Daily Anchors

I committed to doing three things every day:

- Meditate for twenty minutes.

- Go to yoga and pay attention to the nonphysical teachings in the class. Or read a few pages from the large pile of books about spirituality, kindness, meaning, and self-compassion that I was quickly accumulating.

- Continue my gratitude practice, including having one positive and kind interaction with another person each day.

I called these my daily anchors. (As we explore different happier practices in part 2, I am going to ask you to create your own daily anchors.) Every morning I would write them at the top of my to-do list. After a few weeks I added two other ones: do something nice for me and *be here now*, be present with myself exactly as I was. Janet had been talking about me being kinder to myself, so while I still thought I hadn't earned that yet, putting it on my to-do list made it a little more real. And while it was still scary to me, I wanted to try to be with my thoughts and feelings, even for short moments, rather than do what I had always done—run away, escape, and distract myself. That was the idea behind *Be. Here. Now.* which I often used as a reminder, literally saying those words to myself when I caught my mind trying to escape the present moment.

## Be. Here. Now.

We'll explore strategies for handling difficult emotions in chapter 6, but here is a first step you can take now. It's simple and yet profound at the same time. The next time you feel something you don't want to feel, whether it's stress, regret, anxiety, sadness, or something else, try to stay with that feeling for a little bit, even if for just a minute. Say to yourself, "be here now." Use these words to help yourself remain with the feeling rather than distracting yourself or otherwise shutting it down. Notice yourself looking for an immediate way to escape it, and decide to do something different. Notice how you feel. You may discover that as you do this, you come to fear this feeling a bit less or experience it with less intensity.

I told Janet about my new daily practice. Months later she told me that the only way I was able to get through this dark and difficult period in my life—a spiritual crisis, as she called it—was because of my discipline and tenacity to stick with practicing my daily anchors.

"Where you are today compared to where you were—well, that's a miracle," she said. "But miracles aren't passive. They aren't magic. A true miracle takes work and practice and some faith. You didn't have much faith at first, but you were extremely tenacious and dedicated to doing the work. And you didn't give up."

"At the beginning, my faith was in you," I told her, smiling. I didn't need to tell Janet just how much she had helped me—she could see it—but it felt so good to do it. Then I took out a small piece of paper and wrote down:

**Miracle = Faith + Practice**

While *faith* and *miracle* were new to my vocabulary and still a little uncomfortable, practice had long been something I could get behind. I was learning. And that is what my daily anchors became, my daily practice to find my path out of what felt like complete inner darkness.

I kept notes about my daily anchors practice in a journal on my computer. Reading through it while writing this book was like meeting an old friend I hadn't seen in a long time. It was really painful, but I also felt so proud of how far I've come. It truly seemed like a miracle that the scared, desperate person who wrote those words could be here now as someone who feels more peaceful, hopeful, joyful, and present with all the parts of her life. But I also wished I could run back and hug that version of me and tell her to go a little easier on herself.

## My Journal

**DAY 1**

This feels like the END. End of my life, end of something. Why does it feel this way? IT'S AWFUL.

**DAY 9**

Maybe I'll go into the woods and meditate for the rest of my life, like Michael Singer in *The Surrender Experiment*. Wait, I can't do that; I have a kid and a mortgage. Also, I can't meditate.

**DAY 15**

Opened my eyes this morning and it was like this insane tsunami of anxiety, this feeling of I CAN'T TAKE ANOTHER MORNING LIKE THIS! Went downstairs to try to meditate. Total failure. But at least I sat there.

**DAY 22**

It is exhausting how I talk to myself all the time. Like, a constant pep talk. "Be here now. It's okay to be how you are. You deserve to be kind to yourself. You don't need to achieve more, you're enough. It's okay to feel like everything is a mess." It helps, but my God, how long will I have to do this?

**DAY 26**

I'm at the Summit conference in Utah. It's like a completely different world. Everyone here uses the word *soul*. Yet they are also smart and creative and successful. What!? On a hike, talking to this guy Adam about dealing with my storms, and how I'm doing things I never thought I would, like meditation, etc. Testing whether I could be honest. He didn't even blink; he just told me about some of his challenges. It's so totally new to me to actually have these honest conversations.

**DAY 29**

Clearly have lost my mind because today I had an astrology reading. And, get this, she said: "It's like you're trying to prove your worth. And you think, 'okay, I'm making this long list of things that prove my worth until God notices me.' And then you realize it's all a cosmic joke. There is no God. *You* are it. You decide. There is no one to check your list, no one to prove your worth to." How could she know this?

**DAY 34**

Thirty days of sitting down to meditate every morning. It's literally like an anchor, keeps me grounded even when I can't calm my thoughts. I AM SOMEONE WHO MEDITATES.

**DAY 40**

In the meditation workshop today the teacher quoted someone whose name I forget but I loved the saying: the purpose of meditation is not to feel a certain way, it is to feel how you feel. THIS! Except holy crap I don't always want to know how I feel!?

**DAY 53**

I feel like a child learning to listen to myself. Feels dumb, feels like something I should have learned to do way earlier in life. But OMFG the voice in my head is so mean!

**DAY 57**

Saw Ken for lunch today. He said I seemed different, lighter, less intense. In a good way. I wrote a talk today in an hour and it feels like the best talk I've ever written and more honest. Is this what Janet means when she says once I move from my true self the work will flow differently?

**DAY 60**

Craziest thing: Today was a rough day and yet I feel okay. Not great, but okay. Had stressful meetings and didn't love yoga class, then Avi and I had a tough convo and I yelled at Mia, for which I hated myself. But this is the crazy part: I feel okay, right now, in this moment, I am okay even though this day sucked.

There it is, Day 60. When I wrote this entry I hadn't yet realized just how huge this insight was: I was basically okay even when things sucked. It would take many more months of doing my daily anchors for them to feel natural to me, months of fighting with my ego—which, of course, was still screaming at me for being a cop-out—and learning how to be with my feelings instead of trying to escape them.

But I was learning to allow myself to feel grateful for some moments in my day and accept that there would be other moments when I felt sad, confused, scared, or upset. To not feel like a failure when I couldn't make everything work out the way I felt it *should*, and to allow for the possibility that some things were outside my control. To treat myself with a bit of compassion when I didn't feel how I thought I should feel or when the voice in my head was stuck in a negative spin that I couldn't turn around.

The other revelation was that my life had *not*—and would not—become some amazing dream just because I'd achieved something that meant the world to me, like launching Happier, or learning how to be more present in the moment. The challenges I was facing at work and home were still there with all their complexity and difficulty. I didn't have clear solutions or ideas for how to make every single thing better. But I learned to embrace more of my life as it was. And to my total amazement, the very act of learning that I *could* be okay even when things were not okay—or not as I thought they should be—brought me the contentment that I had been chasing feverishly for more than two decades.

## Learning to Be Happier Now

About a year after I started my journey through the darkness I began to feel that this new way of living—treating myself with more compassion, not always fighting my reality and my emotions, not feeling as if I constantly had to earn the right to feel good by achieving the next amazing milestone—*was* my new reality. I no longer considered it an escape or a resignation from "real" life. I felt as if I had moved from gingerly walking on a swaying tightrope to stepping more confidently along a wider, more forgiving path. My daily anchors ceased to feel like a temporary life jacket to get me out of a crisis and more like a nonnegotiable, regular part of my day.

I felt more comfortable with myself and more present in my life, with Mia, Avi, our family, and friends. Avi and I hadn't magically fixed our marriage but we were starting to melt the thick layer of ice we'd let form between us. We had hope, just like I had fresh new hope for Happier and for myself.

There were still many storms in my life, but I was more okay within them than I had ever been. I had discovered a skill that I'd been missing all these years. It wasn't just gratitude, which is still hugely important and which I still practice as one of my core daily anchors because science doesn't lie (it works!). I had discovered the ability without which we can't experience the genuine, lasting, deep sense of happiness or live fully and be present in all the moments of our lives. I had discovered the importance of learning how be okay even when not everything was okay.

I know from the thousands of Happier emails, messages, and conversations that many of us struggle to reach an impossible state of perfect happiness, hoping that one more achievement or the next important milestone will be the one that delivers the gold. As we hang our hopes of feeling happy somewhere out there in the future, we often rob ourselves of the little moments of connection, enjoyment, and beauty that are already here, within our days. We don't pause enough to truly be present for them because we approach them as simply a means to an end, stepping-stones on our way to our future goal. Even when we do notice them, they often pale in comparison to this place of perfect happiness that we believe awaits us in the future if we work hard enough to get there, if we make everything in our lives just so, if we clear the obstacles in our way.

By relaxing our impossibly high expectations of reaching peak happiness, void of challenges or difficult emotions, we give ourselves permission to experience the joy, kindness, meaning, and contentment in the everyday moments of our lives. When we become present to them, we honor them, and, in turn, they fill us with many of the same emotions we'd been hoping to feel once we reached our happiness goal. We begin to struggle less with our feelings and ourselves because we no longer feel the pressure to turn our "negative" emotions into "positive" ones. Not only do we learn that it's not always possible but also that it's not the goal, because being happier doesn't mean always feeling positive.

Rather, genuine and lasting happiness comes from embracing the rich emotional fabric of our real lives—including the many difficult emotions that we might want to avoid—and learning from, growing, and thriving because of it. Of course it feels awesome to experience joy, fun, or excitement. But it also feels awesome to work toward a meaningful goal, even if we have to encounter tons of stress and disappointment in the process. It feels awesome to feel strong and resilient after working through a difficult situation rather than trying to escape from it because we fear the emotions it brings up.

It sounds strange, but in our efforts to not experience "negative" emotions we miss out on feeling happier. Allowing ourselves to feel the potential stress and fear of a challenging situation and then getting through it brings us great satisfaction and even pride. The joy is in the doing, in the striving, in the effort, in connecting to our inner strength and a sense of meaning that helps us get through life's small and big storms. Genuine happiness isn't limited to pleasant feelings. It's deeper and more encompassing of our complex and beautiful humanity.

Giving up the expectation that we can achieve our way to perfect happiness and broadening our definition of being happier to include not just feeling good but also working through something difficult is incredibly liberating. We can stop running breathlessly ahead, doing more and more and more in hopes of reaching our happiness nirvana. We can stop beating ourselves up for not doing things well enough. We can stop fearing that something bad will happen, and instead savor the good that we have.

We can give ourselves the amazing gift of feeling happier *now*, where we are and how we are, even when not everything is perfect (which is always).

*journal practice*

## I'm Happier Now Because . . .

Revisit your "I'll be happy when . . ." list you made in chapter 1. I have no doubt that everything on that list is meaningful to you. But rather than waiting until you reach those milestones or achieve those accomplishments to feel happy, could you practice finding a few things in your life *as it is* right now that truly make you happier?

Take a few minutes to jot them down in your journal. Begin each one with "I'm happier now because . . ."

It's wonderful to have goals and dreams. In fact, it's so much of what makes us human. But I offer this practice as a way to help you increase your awareness of the moments, experiences, and human connections that bring you joy and meaning. As we will explore together in the coming chapters, doing this doesn't make it less likely that we achieve our goals—quite the opposite. It boosts our ability to achieve our goals and overcome the challenges along the way.

# part 2

Your Daily Anchors for
Becoming Happier Now

# 5

# Developing Your Happier Practice

*How we spend our days is how we spend our lives.*
ANNIE DILLARD

Rachel and I met up on a crisp spring day at Andala Coffee House, my favorite little spot in Cambridge, Massachusetts. Rachel is a photographer; I'd hired her to shoot a workshop of mine some weeks before. During the photo shoot, a smile rarely left her face. She told me about how much she had loved taking photos ever since she got her first camera many years earlier. I loved working with her and wanted to get to know her better. We decided to meet for tea.

As we talked she told me about the beautiful lilacs that were blooming along the street she'd just walked down. When the waiter handed her the small patterned teacup, she held it with care and admired it before she took her first sip. She mentioned that when the Boston metro, called the "T," crosses the Charles River on her commute, she always stops what she's doing—reading or listening to music—to just look out at the water.

She seemed to naturally practice what I speak and write about at Happier: appreciating tiny moments of joy and beauty in our everyday life.

"I don't know if I'm naturally this way," Rachel said when I asked her about it. "I became this way as a necessity, as a way to take care of myself and my son and survive some difficult times."

Rachel is a single mom. Her divorce had been tumultuous, and the relationship right after her divorce had become emotionally abusive. At first, she responded to these painful circumstances by receding into herself. For example, when she was married she stopped listening to any music that truly moved her. She kept some distance between herself and what really mattered to her. Janet might have said that she was keeping distance between her and her true self.

"I spent nearly a decade being emotionally removed from my own feelings and experiences," Rachel told me. "It was how I survived."

After her divorce Rachel began to listen to music she loved again, to take photographs, and to try new things. She was starting to find her way back to her inner light when she fell in love with someone new. Within a few years her new boyfriend became emotionally cruel toward her. When at last she recognized what was happening, it took Rachel time to leave the relationship. She first had to find a new place to live for her and her son.

Rachel told me that, as a mother, giving up wasn't an option. She loved her son and was committed to creating a better life for them both. Circumstances forced her to find ways to be okay in a situation that was far from okay.

"I started to become very mindful of the things that brought me serenity," Rachel told me. "I created a mental tool kit to deal with the constant stream of negativity coming my way. Because I fought for life's little joys sprinkled everywhere, I learned how to deeply experience every flower's scent, every ray of sunshine, every note in songs I liked. Even today, when I pause in these moments, I feel myself filling up with calmness and gratitude. They help to shore up my emotional energy for whatever difficulty comes my way in the course of life."

Embracing her life as it was—leaning into it rather than running away from it, even when it was almost unbearable—didn't come easily to Rachel. She was able to do this because she *practiced*. Rachel had her own set of daily anchors—her "mental tool kit"—that, when she practiced them, helped her feel more okay even when so many things in her life were not.

## Happiness Is a Skill

What Rachel discovered through her experience—and what I learned through mine—is that happiness isn't only a state of mind that we experience but also something that we *do*. It's a skill we can cultivate through practice, just like we can improve our ability to write, play a musical instrument, or cook, for example. It's a skill we can cultivate at *any time*. We don't have to wait until we have done enough, achieved enough, or arranged things in our lives as perfectly as we think they should be. Anyone can practice becoming happier—we don't need to dramatically change our lives or, say, go to Nepal for a year to mediate. The practices that help cultivate our happier skills are simple and don't require more than a few minutes a day.

For me, reframing becoming happier in this way was a life-altering shift. Once I let go of the idea that more hard work and suffering were going to bring me to a state of pure bliss, I could consider what I needed to *do* to be happier *now*, in the present moment. What I realized is that I didn't have to wait for it at all. My daily anchors—these small, simple practices—were the answer. What's more, they worked. To this day they help me cultivate my happier skills when things are going okay and—perhaps most importantly—when they're not.

In the following chapters I will share with you the five core practices that help us build and maintain our happier skills.

These practices are backed by research in psychology and sociology, and the exercises that go with them are inspired by my own experiences, including my study of yoga and meditation. I have taught them to thousands of people through my online courses and in-person workshops and witnessed many people benefit from them. The five core practices are elegantly simple and accessible. They are acceptance, gratitude, intentional kindness, the bigger *why*, and self-care. And their accompanying exercises are simple too. (That's another lesson I've learned: the smallest, simplest actions can have a significant and lasting impact on how we feel, as long as we stick to them.)

Acceptance of our situation and feelings, especially when they're difficult, allows us the clarity to make better decisions about how to move through them. It also helps us feel more peaceful because we don't waste emotional energy fighting how we feel. Instead, we develop confidence in our resilience and ability to get through challenges.

Gratitude helps us experience more moments of joy within the lives we already have, without having to do anything to change them. It helps us counter our brain's frustrating tendency of focusing on the negative, as well as take fewer things for granted.

Being intentionally kind toward other people helps strengthen our human connections so that we feel safe and supported by a meaningful network. Even the tiniest acts of kindness we express toward strangers help humanize our daily experience and bring us joy.

Connecting to our sense of meaning helps us see more of what we do at work and at home as being in service to our higher purpose. This is especially helpful when things are challenging or tedious, and it also helps us feel a deeper satisfaction when things are going well.

Finally, the practice of self-care—nurturing a kinder relationship with ourselves—is essential because it's impossible to feel happier if we're emotionally, spiritually, and physically drained. We'll talk about ways to improve the skills of self-compassion, resting, and finding ways to fuel your soul with creativity.

You might do some of these already. Awesome! But when we bring them together and practice regularly they become an impressive powerhouse that helps us get through tough times and really savor the many good moments that are already in our lives.

*journal practice*

## Creating Your Daily Anchors

Daily anchors are literally that—simple daily practices that help you cultivate your happier skills, even when you're going through small or big life storms. It's easy to start a daily anchors practice. We'll start sketching one out here. This isn't a fixed recipe but rather an opportunity to begin—because we all have to begin somewhere. You can modify it to suit your needs as we explore different practices together in the following chapters, and I'll be here to guide you along the way.

Take out your journal. What are a few things that help you feel more joyful, present, peaceful, and centered? Write them down. At first, just write, don't edit or think about how you would do all these things.

Next, think about which two activities you could realistically commit to doing every day. They need to be fairly simple and not take up a lot of time. An hour-long walk might feel amazing but if you can't do it every day then a twenty-minute walk is a better option

These two activities are the start of your daily anchors practice. Every day, write these daily anchors at the top of your to-do list or wherever you manage your tasks and appointments. (It could be the calendar in your phone, for example.) There's no perfect time of day to do your practices—and you don't have to do them all at the same time—but I have found that the beginning and the end of the day work best for me because that is when I might have a small chunk of time to myself.

Give yourself some time to explore, modify, and change your daily anchors, especially as you start out. Giving each one a week to see if it benefits you is a good amount of time. Resist the impulse to change them daily. Rather, allow them to breathe. Then, if they really aren't doing it for you, switch them up.

As we explore different practices together in the following chapters, I'll ask you to give them a try and add those that work best to your daily anchors list. Be mindful to not make your list too long. The idea isn't to overwhelm yourself with more to-dos but rather to commit to doing a few small things every day that help you feel more content and better able to go through the ups and downs of life with self-compassion and strength. The goal is to feel happier, not more stressed!

## Your Invisible Ally:
## The Emotional Immune System

About a year and a half ago I began to work with a speaking agent to get out and talk to companies and at conferences. He seemed like the perfect partner for this next part of my journey and the growth of Happier. For months and months my agent and I worked together not just to refine my speaking topics and my core points, but also to develop some big ideas for where we could take Happier as a company. With his help I landed some great gigs speaking to large corporate audiences, proof that not only did people want to hear what I had to say but they were also willing to pay for it (whoa!). At that point my speaking fees were the only significant revenue coming into Happier, so this work was key for the company's survival.

Then one day, suddenly, my agent disappeared—he stopped returning my calls, texts, and emails. As I looked back on our work together, I realized that there had been warning signs. I had ignored them because I wanted everything to work out. But even so, I didn't expect to be completely abandoned. It was crushing. Beyond feeling betrayed, I was freaking out about having to rebuild what we had done from scratch. *How much time did I lose? What if Happier runs out of money because I'm not speaking while I look for a new agent? What if no one else wants to work with me? What if it was a fluke that he wanted to work with me and really I'm no good?*

A few days after this happened I had my regular meeting with Janet.

"That's awful," she said when I told her what happened. "How do you feel?"

"This is really terrible," I said. "But I'm okay. Is that crazy?" I was sitting in my favorite plush chair in her sunny office. "I'm nervous about Happier making it on this tight timeline. Things were going so well! It doesn't make any sense! I feel so betrayed. And now I have to find a new agent and grow the speaking gigs all over again, which stresses me out a lot. But I'm not flipping out. I'm not going into a tailspin."

She was smiling. I think she was proud of me.

If the agent had abandoned me a year earlier, I would have been destroyed. Overwhelmed with anxiety and fear, I would have berated myself for not recognizing the warning signs and beaten myself up for being so inept at choosing this guy as my business partner. With such harsh self-talk I wouldn't have been able to function. This situation was, in many ways, my worst-case scenario: just as I saw the light for Happier, and for myself, everything came crashing down. And it would have been my fault, of course. My inner voice would have been sure to remind me.

This time, while I didn't know exactly *how* I would get through this challenge, I had faith that I *could* do it. Not faith in something inexplicable, but faith in my own ability to handle the fear and frustration, just as I had during the previous months. As soon as I accepted my difficult situation and difficult feelings, my emotional immune system offered me the resilience and strength to help me get through them so I could take care of business. By the time my agent disappeared I had been strengthening it for some time with my daily anchors practice. My emotional immune system was helping me get through the storm while I, by practicing, was helping it become stronger.

We often forget that we have this ally. Daniel Gilbert, a Harvard professor and the author of the book *Stumbling on Happiness*, conducted several studies showing that we often overestimate how long and how deeply we'll be affected when something bad happens to us. We forget that we have inner strength to draw on—a psychological immune system, as he calls it—and that if we allow ourselves to experience and process the difficult emotions we feel, we can get through them faster and come out stronger.

Think about it this way: Just as most of us have a physiological immune system that helps protect our body from germs and viruses, our *emotional* immune system helps us get through life's ups and downs. When our bodies are tackling seasonal bugs or occasional infections, they build antibodies, and those antibodies help our entire system fight off other bugs. Similarly, when we allow ourselves to *experience* difficult feelings, our emotional immune system helps us move through them. Each time we do this we improve our ability to do it again—we strengthen our emotional immune system by letting it do its work.

A 2010 study published in the *Journal of Personality and Social Psychology* affirms my own experience. The study found that when we go through adverse experiences, we develop resilience that helps us deal with future challenges. Rather than feeling helpless when we face difficulty or true life trauma, we gain confidence that we can get through it. This confidence in our ability to get through the times when life isn't okay is enormously valuable because it allows us to feel more content and peaceful rather than live in fear of something going wrong.

## Reconnect to Your Strength

Think back to a challenging experience you've gone through. Spend a few moments reflecting and writing about what helped you get through it and the inner strength you might have discovered in yourself.

We often underestimate our resilience. Recalling your ability to persevere through tough times reminds you of the helping hand of your emotional immune system—and your ability to rely on it when times are tough. And this, in turn, helps you to get through future challenges with a bit more ease.

## Overcoming Your Inner Skeptic

None of what I'm sharing with you came easily to me. I've resisted, avoided, dismissed, rolled my eyes, and been outright hostile. Perhaps you know what I'm talking about.

There is a concept in yoga called *samskara*. Our behaviors, words, feelings, and experiences leave emotional and psychological grooves, samskaras. Samskaras can be positive or negative. The more we experience certain thoughts or feelings, the deeper that particular samskaric groove becomes. We can choose which ones to deepen by practicing the actions that cause the feelings we would like to experience more often.

When I first started to learn about this idea in my yoga practice, I was, of course, skeptical. It was counter to the way I thought about emotions. In my mental model, feelings arose spontaneously within us in response to a situation, activity, or experience. While this is still true, we also have the capacity to intentionally cultivate certain feelings.

Other people, including researchers and scientists (perhaps less reflexively skeptical than I am), have fully embraced this idea. One of my favorite examples comes from the work of Amy Cuddy, a professor of social psychology at Harvard University; she shares it in her book *Presence*. You may have seen her awesome TED Talk, "Your Body Language May Shape Who You Are." In it she describes how adopting a superhero pose for just a few minutes—feet a few feet apart, hands on hips, chest slightly forward, chin slightly up—helps increase confidence and reduce fear or anxiety. You may not feel confident going into a big presentation, but physically adopting this pose sends a signal to your brain that you *are* confident. You cultivate the feeling of confidence by taking a certain action, in this case, standing like Wonder Woman or Superman might.

In the same way, the practices we're going to explore together can help you intentionally cultivate feelings of acceptance, gratitude, kindness, purpose, and self-compassion. The more you practice, the easier it becomes to experience those emotions naturally. It's easier to cross-country ski if there are trails in the snow for your skis. It's easier to feel certain emotions if you have created emotional grooves, or samskaras, for them through regular practice. Think of it as "fake it 'til you make it"—do the practices and the feelings will follow. At some point you won't be faking it anymore.

If you catch yourself thinking, as I used to, *This won't work for me* or *I'm too this or that for this to make any difference*, that's absolutely okay. Seriously. There's just one condition: you have to give some of these practices a shot. Even if, at first, it seems as if you're just going through the motions. Try the work and detach from the outcome. What I mean is, relax your expectations about how you *think* you'll feel when you do the practices. Simply take a tiny leap of faith and commit to do them for a certain amount of time, perhaps a week or two. You decide.

## Where You Begin

Take a few minutes to consider why it's important *to you* to cultivate your happier skills. Consider how you feel and how you might want to feel differently. To know if you're making progress as you try the different practices, it's good to know your baseline, where you started.

Here are a few questions you might want to use as jumping-off points:

- Are you constantly stressed out?
- Do small annoyances seem to quickly throw you off your center?
- Do you want to feel more joy, peace, and inner contentment?

- Are you having trouble dealing with difficult people in your life?
- Do you feel you're running from one to-do to another with rarely a moment to catch your breath?
- Are you often harsh with yourself?
- Do friends and family members tell you to go easy on yourself?
- Have you lost touch with what brings you joy or a sense of purpose?

As you go through the book and try some of the practices, come back to what you have written here, as a reminder of where you began and the reason you undertook this journey in the first place. Keep these thoughts fresh to hold you accountable and help you stick to the practices, even on days when you don't feel like it or when your inner skeptic is very loud.

You might also consider keeping notes in your journal as you undertake your daily anchors practice. When I reread my daily anchors journal many months after I wrote it, I realized that I'd done myself a huge favor by writing down my feelings and my progress. Whenever the voice in my head tries to shift me off my path, or I fall into fear or doubt, I reread some of my entries. They remind me about how far I've come thanks to my commitment to my daily anchors and fill me with energy to get back to cultivating my happier skills.

## Nataly's Pep Talk

You're important enough to be happier. You do deserve it—now, at this point in your life, just the way you are. You're not too busy to cultivate happier skills because these practices rarely take more than a few minutes. And you don't have to *earn* the right to live fully in all moments of your life to be filled with more joy and spark and a sense of peace. Just invest some of your attention and intention in the practices and see what happens.

Choosing another way to live, not the desperate chase of nonexistent perfect happiness, literally saved my life—including my family, my work, my creativity, and my spirit. It also made my daily life experience so much brighter, fuller, richer, more authentic, more real, more filled with kindness, joy, and contentment. Yes, I still have fear at times. But I'm less afraid of my emotions because I'm also confident that I'll be okay when I experience them and that even when life throws me into small or big storms, I can rely on my daily anchors and my strengthened emotional immune system. I can't tell you how incredibly life-affirming it is to be fully present for all the moments of my life.

Even if you're skeptical as you read the following chapters, I'm certain that if you do the practices—and I mean really do them rather than just read about them—you'll notice a difference in how you feel. You'll notice how present you are in the small moments of your days, even when they're tough. You'll notice how small moments of joy reveal themselves naturally and easily. You'll notice that you can be okay even when things aren't going your way.

But don't take my word for it. Try it out for yourself.

Here is the deal: if you truly give these practices a shot—you really dig into them for a few weeks—and you don't notice any positive impact, email me. My personal email is natalyk@happier.com. Tell me what you practiced and what didn't work, and we'll see if we can't figure it out together. Yes, I'm completely serious about offering to do this. Perhaps that is another hint at how passionately confident I am about the power of these practices.

# Happier Now Pledge

Start your journey to being happier now by making the Happier Now Pledge. It's a declaration of your commitment to *yourself*, but also to the people around you and especially to those you care about. As you'll discover, the magic of being happier is that it doesn't just affect you. Your sense of well-being affects everyone around you. You don't have to do anything to them or with them, you just have to work on yourself.

Read through the pledge on the following page. You can even read it out loud. If you're doing these practices with a friend or partner—or a group of friends or colleagues—you may decide to read the pledge to each other and sign it in each other's presence. If you're doing it solo, that is great too. Read it, make it your own, sign it, and take a photo of it or type it up and put it somewhere where you can see it often, perhaps on your bathroom mirror or next to your computer. (Feel free to have some fun decorating it so that it really speaks to you!)

It would bring me great joy to see your Happier Now Pledge! I encourage you to take a photo of it—however you like, including perhaps with your beautiful, smiling face next to it—and share it with me and thousands of other awesome humans who are undertaking this journey at the same time as you. In sharing your pledge, you might also inspire someone who hasn't yet made the commitment to take the first step. What a gift that would be.

We'll share some of your pledges on happier.com and on our social media channels to help inspire others to take their own Happier Now Pledge. Here are the ways you can share the photo of your pledge:

- Share it on Instagram, Facebook, or Twitter with the hashtag #happiernow.
- Email it to pledge@happier.com.

# Happier Now Pledge

**I pledge to give myself permission to . . .**

- Stop striving for perfection (in my life and myself).
- Not always be okay (or pretend to be okay).
- Accept my emotions with courageous compassion.
- Embrace all the moments in my life—the good, the bad, and the in between.

**I pledge to practice being happier now and to . . .**

- Honor even the smallest moments with gratitude and delight in the ordinary.
- Be intentionally kind without expecting anything in return.
- Infuse my bigger *why* into my days (and hold on to it when I struggle).
- Treat myself with compassion and care.

**I am enough.**

- I don't have to earn the right to feel happier.
- My well-being isn't an extra—it's my responsibility to myself and people I love.
- Through my happier practice I become the force of good in the world.

**I commit to being happier now because:**

_____

_____

_____

_____

DATE | SIGNATURE

# Find Your Happier Now Ally

When I began my journey toward learning how to be happier now, one of the most helpful things was having a few people to whom I was accountable. My teacher Janet was one, and Mia, my daughter, became another ally. When I shared with her that I felt guilty taking time to take care of myself, she loudly proclaimed that it would make her happy to see me happier. So doing things that fuel me was my responsibility not just to myself but also to her. (Don't you sometimes hate when kids say the wisest things?)

Consider nominating your own Happier Now Ally. It can be a family member, friend, coworker—anyone who will remind you to stick to your practice when the voice in your head gets a bit too harsh; a person whose words you may sometimes hear more clearly than your own. It's a gift to be able to help someone (we'll talk about this in the chapter about intentional kindness), so I'm certain that the person you ask to be your ally will love the chance to be there to help you find more joy, meaning, kindness, contentment, and acceptance within the moments of your days.

Here is the pledge I've created for your Happier Now Ally to sign. (You can take a photo of it and send it to your ally so they can sign it.)

# Happier Now Ally Pledge

**I hereby promise to:**

- Encourage and support you as you practice being happier now.
- Remind you that you're worth your own love, care, and compassion.
- Tell you that it's okay to not be okay and to screw up . . .
- . . . as long as you get back to your practice.

**I'm here to be your ally, your cheerleader, and your unwavering supporter as you go on this journey.**

**Your practice will not just help you, but also me and so many other people in your world because the more you practice, the more joy, kindness, meaning, peace, and compassion you'll share with all of us. Remember that.**

_____

DATE | SIGNATURE

# 6

# Acceptance

Acceptance of the present moment has nothing to
do with resignation in the face of what's happening.
It simply means a clear acknowledgement that what is
happening is happening. Acceptance doesn't tell you what
to do. What happens next, what you choose to do, that
has to come out of your understanding of the moment.

JON KABAT-ZINN

A few minutes after flight 1549 took off from New York City's LaGuardia Airport, a flock of geese struck both of its engines. Both of them failed. Just 209 seconds passed between the time of impact and the moment when Captain Chesley "Sully" Sullenberger safely landed the plane on the Hudson River, saving the lives of 150 passengers and five crew members on board. It was the first such landing in history, now sometimes called "the miracle on the Hudson."

After the incident, I caught an interview with Captain Sullenberger. While recounting the tense moments in the cockpit with his copilot, he talked about how seeing the flock of birds approach helped him handle the emergency. As soon as the engines failed, he realized it was from the collision with the birds and didn't waste precious seconds wondering what might have happened. He was startled, of course, and fully aware of the peril they were in, but he immediately shifted his attention to figuring out what to do next. While he didn't use these exact words, what he practiced in that moment was acceptance.

What does it mean to practice acceptance?

It means that you're able to surrender to the present moment and witness it *as it is*, not colored by your past experience with similar moments or your desire for how this moment *should* be.

## The Valley of Suffering

So often I can trace my unhappiness to wanting things to be different than they are. *That's not how it should be* likes to swirl around in my head. How often do you catch yourself thinking something like:

- This vacation isn't going how I think it *should* be.

- The weather isn't as warm as it *should* be.

- My job isn't as interesting as it *should* be.

- My friend/partner/colleague isn't being as kind to me as they *should* be.

- This traffic/subway isn't moving as fast as it *should* be.

We create a story, a vision about how something should happen, and then when it doesn't pan out that way we feel frustrated, disappointed, and even angry. This tendency is a close cousin of our inclination to come up with "I'll be happy when . . ." scenarios. We envision a set of narrow conditions under which we'll feel happy and expect ourselves and the world to perfectly execute them. It's like saying:

- I'm *only* going to be happy when this vacation goes exactly how I want it to go.

- I'm *only* going to be happy when my friends are as kind to me as I want them to be.

- I'm *only* going to be happy when my commute goes the way that I expect it to.

We don't feel good when reality fails to meet our expectations. That is natural. But it's another thing to get stuck in the Valley of Suffering, the space between how something is and how we have decided it should be. The crazy thing is that this Valley of Suffering is entirely our own creation: *we* create the narrowly defined conditions for our happiness in our minds, which means that we basically *choose* to limit our happiness. But we also have the power to clear a path out of the Valley of Suffering—by practicing acceptance.

It's both funny and sad at the same time, right? We literally reduce our own ability to feel good by creating a bunch of requirements that need to be met first. But we can learn from this tendency. By practicing acceptance—meeting reality *as it is* and softening our judgment of how we think it *should* be—we give ourselves a lot more surface area in which to find happiness, maybe even happiness we never could have expected.

Without a doubt, Captain Sullenberger wished that the birds hadn't flown into the plane. He probably wished that he didn't have to decide how to save the people on the flight—and himself. I can't even grasp how intense the pressure was that he was feeling. But he didn't have the luxury of getting stuck in the Valley of Suffering. He faced the situation as it was and then moved on to figure out what he could do about it. Can you imagine what might have happened if he had wasted some of the 209 seconds by getting angry that the flight wasn't going smoothly or being upset that he had to figure out a solution?

For most of us, getting stuck in the Valley of Suffering isn't a life or death choice. It's almost never as urgent as it was for Captain Sullenberger. But consider how much you deplete your emotional and physical energy every day by battling with reality. My Achilles' heel is the weather. I enjoy my long daily walks much more when it's warm and sunny than when it's cold and rainy. (Who doesn't?) I just really don't like the cold. (Yes, I know. I grew up in Russia where it was freezing cold for many months of the year, but I'm a total wuss when it comes to being cold.) So late spring, summer, and early fall are my favorite seasons. But I live in Boston where the weather can be unpredictable. We can have sixty-degree days in February and fifty-degree days in June.

When the weather is colder or rainier than normal, when it's not the weather I was hoping for, I drive myself crazy. I look up temperature and rainfall averages. I read the *Farmers' Almanac* to try to figure out why it's not as warm as it should be. I look at charts comparing the number of sunny days in Boston with other areas. I read articles analyzing weather patterns. It's completely ridiculous. I put myself in the Valley of Suffering because the weather, something completely outside of my control, isn't as I think it should be. It's as if I believe that being frustrated about the weather could improve it or how I feel about it—which, of course, is nuts. But fighting with reality feels like doing *something* while accepting it can feel like giving up.

Meditation teacher Michael Singer writes in his book *The Surrender Experiment* that surrendering is *not* doing nothing or giving up but rather a way to clearly see what is happening.

He writes: "The practice of surrender was actually done in two, very distinct steps: first, you let go of the personal reactions of like and dislike that form inside your mind and heart; and second, with the resultant sense of clarity, you simply look to see what is being asked of you by the situation unfolding in front of you."

When we practice acceptance we transcend our feelings about the situation so we can witness it clearly. By doing this we gain the ability to choose how to act rather than simply react. If I learn to accept that Boston's weather will always be unpredictable and sometimes colder than normal for the season, then I can choose to do some things to make it more bearable, like not put away my warmer coats and scarves early in the spring so I can easily grab them on the chillier days.

In a way, acceptance is the opposite of resignation. It allows us the chance to make an intentional choice about how to approach something that we can't avoid. It's empowering to decide to be in the driver's seat, to have that choice. Sometimes, much to our surprise, it can lead us to discover a path we hadn't even considered.

My friend Ken had been working on his start-up for several years—a dating app in which women would recommend their guy friends for dates with other women—until he couldn't raise additional funding. Without it he couldn't invest in marketing his app or adding features it needed. I watched Ken struggle with this reality for more than a year. He believed in his product and wanted to make it work, but he was constantly frustrated by not having enough capital to help it grow. As a fellow entrepreneur, I could feel Ken's pain—when you create something you love, you don't ever want to give up trying to make it work. Ever. But eventually, Ken realized that he couldn't change the situation. Without more users, he couldn't raise more money, and without raising more money, he couldn't gain more users. It was difficult, but he put his start-up on hold and took some time to decompress, catch his breath, and think about what he wanted to do next. (If you're curious, yes, I did talk his ear off about trying out some of my daily anchors practices that helped me get through my dark time.)

A few months later Ken and I caught up for coffee and he excitedly told me what he was up to. He had decided to finally pursue something he had always loved: making videos to share ideas that inspire people. I'd known Ken for ten years but had no clue that this was his passion. "You're a catalyst for this decision, you know?" he told me, with his signature smile. "You helped my own surrender experiment by sharing yours—and telling me to read *The Surrender Experiment*!"

I know how difficult it was for Ken to accept the reality that his app wasn't going to reach the potential he saw for it. I've been in his shoes several times. But by surrendering to the reality and moving past his feelings of sadness and frustration, Ken was able to gain clarity about what to do next. He wasn't held back by his disappointment. He found what he was truly passionate about and what he wanted to pour his energy into.

That is one of the biggest gifts of acceptance. It helps us redirect our emotional and psychological energy so that we can make decisions that better serve us and ultimately the people around us. We pay an emotional cost when we spend time on the "woulda, coulda, shoulda" scenarios. It takes energy to be upset that the weather isn't as nice as it should be, that your job isn't as challenging as you wish it were, that your project or company isn't growing as fast as it should be. As human beings we don't have unlimited reserves of energy. When we spend it in the Valley of Suffering, we have less of it to devote to moving through it and improving our situation.

## Leaving the Valley of Suffering

Think of something that is causing you to be stuck in the Valley of Suffering—something that is not how you wish it were. For example, maybe you're beating yourself up for not being in as good of shape as you wish you were. Or a friend is not being as kind to you as you think they should be.

Now, complete this sentence in your journal: "I'm not happy that [insert what is causing you to be in the Valley of Suffering], but this is how it is right now."

I know this is difficult, but remember that seeing something clearly and accepting it does not mean never changing it. Just the opposite, actually. Once you've written your sentence, practice truly accepting how things are, including how you feel. I am not asking you to like the situation, but to witness it without getting lost in your feelings about it.

Next, write down one or two things you can do to improve the situation. Perhaps you decide to commit to a daily walk or download an app to help you eat healthier. Or you will reach out to your friend rather than waiting for them to be kind to you. Make these steps small and concrete, so you can focus your attention on them and truly commit to doing them.

This practice will help to shift your emotional energy from being stuck in the Valley of Suffering to taking steps to move beyond it.

## Overcoming the Fear of Feeling Bad

A few months ago I received this email from Jana, a member of the Happier community, sharing with me how accepting a shocking and dramatic change in her life led her to discover new ways to cultivate joy:

After years of purposefully living a healthy lifestyle, yet feeling awful, living in denial and trying to convince myself that everything was wonderful, I received a diagnosis of a chronic incurable illness. "But I'm doing everything right!" I yelled. "This is not how it should be!" At first I focused on what was wrong. I learned all I could about this illness and how it affected me. I wailed. I became frustrated and angry and sad. I grieved the loss of my previous life.

But somewhere in the grieving and trying to track patterns and understand what was going on, I learned to accept what was happening and began to find gratitude and to focus on the positive. No more about what I can't do. I started exploring what I can do. What I can still do and what I can now do that I had never tried before.

In many ways, my world has become smaller because of this illness. But I know myself better now than before. I accept things as they are, try to improve what I can, and focus on what works, not on what's wrong and can never be fixed. As I continue to accept things as they are, focus on the positive, and discover new ways to be in the world, I can say I am happier now than I've ever been.

I was touched by Jana's courageous acceptance of something that obviously turned out very differently than how she wished it would. It also struck me that before she was able to accept her situation, she spent time grieving it, feeling sad and angry about it. And before she allowed herself to *feel* those very difficult emotions, she first had to be okay with having them in the first place.

Many of us are afraid not just of the emotions themselves but of admitting, even to ourselves, that we're experiencing anything "negative." I know I did. For the longest time I felt that if I admitted to myself that I felt pain, sadness, or fear, then I would get stuck in those feelings forever. If I allowed myself to accept that something wasn't okay, I was resigning myself to the fact that it would never get better. But researchers have found that many of us overestimate the permanence of painful emotions. In *Flourish*, Martin Seligman writes about how we bounce back from feeling sad, upset, angry, or frustrated quicker than we anticipate. Like Daniel Gilbert, the Harvard psychologist I mentioned in chapter 5, has suggested, we forget about our ally, our emotional immune system, that gives us the resilience to get through difficult times if we allow ourselves to feel the difficult emotions that come with them.

Many of us fear losing a loved one. In *Option B*, which she cowrote with Adam Grant, Facebook's COO Sheryl Sandberg writes about suddenly losing her husband of eleven years. The idea of life forever without Dave was paralyzing, and the pain almost indescribable. To make it worse, she wasn't just grief-stricken; she was grief-stricken about being grief-stricken. She didn't want to feel the way she did. Who can blame her?

The rabbi who led Dave's funeral advised Sheryl to "lean into the suck." He warned her that it would be terrible, but leaning in would make the awful feelings pass faster. The rabbi was right: it was terrible. Yet the more Sheryl allowed herself to experience those awful feelings, the less she was surprised by them. She took crying breaks, sometimes in her car, sometimes in the bathroom at work (her kids learned to do this too). "When I stopped fighting those moments, they passed more quickly," she writes.

As I was reading Sheryl's words, I had an insight into why I'd resisted the idea of acceptance for so long. I used to think that *accepting* was the same as *liking* something. So how was it ever possible to like something tragic, such as sickness, misfortune, or death? Did acceptance require me to become callous and inhumane?

Eventually, I realized that acceptance has nothing to do with liking the situation. In fact, "leaning into the suck" asks that we not judge things and feelings according to our preferences but rather witness them from a more neutral point of view, like an impartial observer. At first this can be difficult to do. It can feel insensitive, ridiculous, and impossible, especially when the situation we're trying to accept involves pain or loss. But as Sheryl's experience teaches us, the first step forward is to accept the bare fact of how something *is*. Dave *had* died. Jana *did* have a chronic, incurable illness. I *had* been a refugee living in the projects outside Detroit, getting made fun of by my classmates because I couldn't really speak English. It doesn't mean we forget or bury the pain, sadness, or fear. It means that even if something is heartbreaking, we allow for a tiny space to open where we can take a breath.

Sometimes it seems that if we acknowledge that we're having "negative" emotions, we're admitting defeat. We have failed at doing life right and we're doomed to never feel good again. Unless we feel good, upbeat, and positive, we're doing something wrong.

We live in a society, especially in America, where we're expected to manage our emotions and shift the negative into the positive. "Don't cry, have a cookie. Don't be angry, have a toy," says my friend Emily Fletcher, who runs Ziva Meditation, a meditation studio in New York. "We hear this all the time. We've been trained since childhood to not feel our feelings because it makes other people uncomfortable. We've been taught to not feel what we feel if it's not something good."

I hadn't considered this perspective, but she's right. We're taught from an early age that we should feel happy. We should control our negative emotions, get over them, and move on. Once we judge certain emotions in our life as negative, once we label them with our emotional label maker, anytime we experience them, we feel as if we're doing something wrong.

So we try to avoid them, we fear them, we use all means possible to distract ourselves. While I'm not against feeling good, I know all too well that the pressure to feel good can lead us down a frustrating path toward feeling the opposite.

The first time I allowed myself to start to accept that I was filled with painful feelings was with Janet. I thought the earth would open up and swallow me.

"I just feel so hopeless," I said. Then, immediately, I panicked. It felt terrible to hear myself say those words. It was like a period at the end of my life, an end: *She worked hard but she failed, and now she is hopeless! Loser! Weak! Pathetic! Giving up!*

"Of course you do," Janet said, nodding. "Of course right now you feel hopeless. It's okay."

I expected her to tell me that soon I would feel better. But she didn't. I expected her to give me things to do to feel less hopeless. She didn't. I expected her to tell me reasons why I shouldn't feel hopeless in the first place. She didn't. She just sat there in acceptance of how I felt, giving me space to feel it.

It wasn't immediate, but as the days and weeks progressed, as I worked through the pile of painful emotions I'd tried to suppress, I realized that accepting them wasn't the period at the end of a sentence. It wasn't the end. It was the beginning.

By accepting that you feel something that you think is negative or difficult—just by clearly seeing it—you allow for the possibility that at some point you'll be able to make choices about it rather than being victim to your circumstances or emotions. I spoke about this with Susan David, a psychologist on the faculty of Harvard Medical School and the author of *Emotional Agility: Get Unstuck, Embrace Change, and Thrive in Work and Life.* She said that when we experience a difficult feeling and try to resist it, it's as if we're wrestling with it, playing a version of tug-of-war: *Should I feel this? I shouldn't feel this! I'm wrong to feel this, but what do I do? I feel it.*

"You're wasting energy and you're invalidating yourself while you do this," Susan told me. "But when you breathe into 'this is what I'm feeling,' and you notice it with courage, there is incredible learning and insight that can come from that space."

Sabrina has been my dental hygienist for the past ten years. Almost every time she comes out to the waiting room to greet me, she has a bright smile on her face. About a year ago, when I asked her how she was doing, she replied differently than usual.

"I'm feeling really stressed. Overwhelmed. And I don't know why I feel this way. I mean, my life is really great. I have great kids, I love my husband, I have a good job, my family is nearby. But I just don't seem to feel good, you know?"

This was the first time I ever heard her say anything other than "Everything is great!"

Sabrina knows that my work is about helping people feel happier so I think what I said next surprised her.

"It's okay not to feel good sometimes, even if everything feels like it's in the right place," I told her. "I used to put pressure on myself to always be upbeat and it seemed like that's what everyone expected from me. But in the past few years I've tried to go a little easier on myself, to let myself not have to be positive all the time. It's been a big relief."

"But I've always been this really happy person," Sabrina insisted. "In high school everyone would always say, 'When we see you, you always have a smile on your face!' I usually do! So I don't know why I don't feel good now."

When Sabrina was done cleaning my teeth, I suggested she be a little kinder to herself. "Don't beat yourself up so much when you don't feel happy. It's okay to not feel okay—you don't need to try so hard to come out of feeling that way quickly," I told her.

Six months later I was back for my regular cleaning. Sabrina greeted me with her usual warm smile, and once I settled into the chair I asked her how she was doing.

"I feel a lot better. I've tried to just go with the flow a little more, to not push myself so hard, to be nicer to myself, like you said. And the weird thing is I actually lost a bunch of weight without doing anything more. It's like, when I got lighter inside I got lighter on the outside." (Sabrina had talked about trying to lose the last stubborn ten pounds after her pregnancy.)

As she talked I noticed that Sabrina's face looked more relaxed. Everything about her seemed more at ease, less at attention. I was so happy to hear her words that—I couldn't help it, I gave her a big hug.

I knew all too well the pressure that Sabrina felt to be happy, happy, happy all the time. For most of my life I was terrified to admit that I felt any other way but great. It felt both like a sign of failing at life and disappointing others—everyone expected me to be super energetic and happy, it seemed. I know I'm not the only one to feel this way. After I began to slowly "come out" to friends about some of the turmoil I felt inside, so many of them told me that they were afraid to disappoint people in their lives by admitting to not feeling good or optimistic. They felt that others depended on their upbeat, sparkly happiness for their own well-being.

One time, when I was starting to drown (it seemed) in the pain I'd tried to contain for so many years, I had lunch with my best friend, Sharon.

She could sense that I was still holding on tightly to my old way of being, to pretend I was happy and good and nothing else. I was still trying to control what and how I felt. As friends do, she didn't try to convince me to do otherwise. Instead, she asked me what I needed to allow myself to just feel what I was feeling.

"I don't know, permission from God? Okay, I don't really believe in God, but something huge like that—permission from the universe!"

We laughed, but we both knew that I was as serious as I was kidding. I needed permission to feel how I felt, to allow myself to experience all the painful emotions I'd been avoiding. That night I found a card from Sharon in our mailbox:

Dear Nataly,

I know that you asked me to get permission from God, but I had some difficulties in communication, mainly from my end.

So how about I give you the permission? I know it's not your first choice, but let me try.

Here I go!

I give you permission:

> To be angry
> To be sad
> To not know for sure who you are
> To be loved
> To trust
> To let it go

I give you the permission to call Sharon on the phone even if you hate the phone.

I give you permission to sleep tonight because it will be okay.

LOVE, SHARON

Sharon's card is one of my most treasured possessions. I keep it in the drawer of my nightstand, next to the many cards my daughter and husband have written to me over the years. I cry-smile every time I read it. It's my permission to be okay when I'm not okay and a small reminder that I can lean into the suck and know that I'll get through it.

You deserve to give yourself this permission, too, to experience difficult feelings without fear or judgment. By doing that you create a path through them.

# Permission
# Slip

In your journal, write yourself a permission slip to feel how you feel, no changes required. Whenever you get stuck thinking that what you're feeling is wrong or not what you should be feeling, go back and reread it.

Here is some inspiration to get you started. But be creative and have fun making this practice your own as well.

Dear me,

This permission slip entitles you to feel however you feel, at any time and without any obligations to change it or modify it. However you feel is absolutely okay.

Take your time feeling what you feel. You might think it's "wrong" or you might feel uncomfortable feeling this way. Heck, it might hurt a lot. I understand.

But I give you permission to feel it anyway. Don't beat yourself up for it. Don't think you're doing anything wrong. You're not. You're a human being with a rich fabric of emotions and you have my permission to feel all of them, including the ones you feel right now.

I LOVE YOU, ME

## The Power of Embracing Difficult Emotions

Difficult emotions like sadness or disappointment don't feel good, which is another reason many of us try to avoid them. Who in the world wants to feel bad? It sucks!

But studies show that when we allow ourselves to acknowledge our feelings and feel what we feel, we reduce the impact and intensity of these emotions. Matthew Lieberman, a professor at the University of California, Los Angeles, conducted a series of brain-imaging studies to demonstrate this. When study participants in a functional MRI machine—it measures brain activity by looking at blood flow—were shown photos of faces expressing strong feelings, their brain signals grew strongest in the amygdala, the part of the brain responsible for generating emotions, including stress and fear. But when researchers asked the study participants to label the emotion they saw in the photo, the activity in the amygdala decreased while activity in the frontal cortex, the area of the brain responsible for emotional processing, increased. The researchers hypothesized that simply labeling an emotion transforms it into something to observe and study. When we acknowledge a feeling, we shift from being in it to witnessing it, and this reduces its intensity.

On the flip side, when we attempt to suppress feelings because we don't want to experience them, we reduce our capacity to get through them. Our emotional immune system can't help us process a challenging emotion unless we first become aware of it, just as our physical immune system can't help us fight off a germ unless it first recognizes it. Not acknowledging a tough feeling cuts us off from our own resilience.

In *Emotional Agility*, Susan David describes a study where researchers asked participants who were trying to quit smoking to avoid trying to control their cravings for cigarettes as they came up: "The program centered on the metaphor of a car journey, with the participant as the driver, heading toward a destination of personal importance—namely, quitting. In the back seat are all the driver's thoughts and emotions, behaving like your bad-influence friends from high school, yelling 'Do it! Go on—just one puff!' and 'You'll never make it, wimp!' Participants in the program are told to allow room for these unruly 'passengers,' while keeping their eye on the prize."

The participants who were assigned to what Dr. David calls the "willingness group"—those who learned to willingly accept and allow the presence of the cravings—had higher rates of quitting smoking than those who participated in the standard program recommended by the National Cancer Institute. When we allow ourselves to experience our cravings or our painful emotions, we reduce the power they have over us.

Acknowledging an emotion also gives us an opportunity to do something else: to learn more about it, why we're experiencing it, and what we might do to shift how we feel. Dr. David has practiced acknowledging difficult feelings herself. She shared with me that on a recent long business trip, she was feeling guilty about spending so much time away from her family.

"Of course, I didn't enjoy feeling that way. But every emotion has a purpose, so I asked myself what I could learn from my guilt. I thought about it for a while and realized that my balance of spending time on work and family was off. That was useful! You see, by allowing myself to feel the guilt rather than try to avoid it, I learned something meaningful and was able to make some shifts in my life that allowed me to spend more time with my family."

When she considered her guilt through a learning lens rather than a damning lens that so many of us default to, Dr. David discovered something important and made a change in her life. It wasn't easy to acknowledge to myself that I felt hopeless (let alone to Janet), but by approaching this emotion through a learning lens I gave myself the chance to dig a little deeper and gain some insight into why I felt how I did. It was one of the paths that led to my realization that I'd hung so much of my self-worth on my achievements that I didn't feel I deserved to feel happy unless I was working nonstop and achieving success.

By accepting that I felt hopeless, I gave myself the space to start to feel hopeful again. By embracing her chronic illness, Jana began to appreciate what she was able to do and try new things. By taking some pressure off herself to always feel good,

Sabrina wasted less energy resisting her stress and felt lighter and less overwhelmed with time. That is the magic of accepting your difficult emotions, experiencing them without avoidance or fear and without becoming overwhelmed or paralyzed by them. In the very act of accepting that you feel how you feel, you create an opportunity to feel better.

*journal practice*

## Embracing Your Stress

Most of us experience stress often, so this is a good exercise to practice. When you're stressed, allow yourself ten to fifteen minutes to feel it. Literally give yourself permission to fully embrace your stress. Take out your journal and write down everything that is stressing you out, big and small. Seeing your stress on paper will help you observe it rather than be overwhelmed by the feeling of it.

## Cultivating Your Inner Witness

We can't accept how something is if we're not present enough to notice it.

During my talks, I ask the audience to join me for two minutes of being still and silent as part of the Five-Minute Happier Workout (shared with you later in the book). I put on a timer and ask everyone to get comfortable and close their eyes. As everyone settles down, I usually say something like the following: "Whatever you think or feel, it's okay. If you're thinking this is the best thing you've done today, that is okay. If you're cursing me for making you do this, that is also okay. The goal of this is not to eliminate all thoughts; that is not possible. It's simply for you to arrive in this place, in this moment, and become aware of your thoughts rather than be carried away by them. Treat your thoughts as something you're reading on a piece of paper in front of you."

A woman named Melissa came up to me after a recent workshop. She seemed eager to tell me something.

"I have tried to meditate a bunch of times before," she told me. "Actually, me and my husband have both tried it. But my thoughts usually run a mile a minute, and I would always just get so frustrated. I would sit there and try to be calm and breathe and all that, but my thoughts would come one after the other. I thought the whole idea was to empty the mind. So I felt like I couldn't do it right."

Boy, could I relate. My early experiments with meditation usually ended with a frustrating feeling that I was a total meditation failure because I couldn't free my mind of thoughts and feel a deep sense of inner peace (or, let's be honest, *any* inner peace). Whenever I'd see images of people meditating, they all looked perfectly serene, so naturally I assumed that they had figured out how to quiet their thoughts while I had failed.

I gained the insight I now share with my audiences at a meditation workshop led by a Hindu monk. "The purpose of your meditation practice is not to eliminate all thoughts, but to learn to observe your thoughts and to create some distance between you and your thoughts so you can increase your awareness of how you feel," he told us.

This was extremely liberating. In fact, it helped me establish a regular meditation practice. Some days I sit down on my meditation cushion in the morning and my mind races with thought after thought for the entire twenty minutes of my practice. Other days, my thoughts are less frazzled and slower. But the critical skill that meditation has helped me hone is my awareness that my thoughts are racing, or frazzled, or less frazzled, or even peaceful. This helps me gain some insight into how I'm feeling and make better decisions about what to do about it: acknowledge certain thoughts and emotions, dig a little deeper into them, or recognize that they aren't helpful and let them go.

"I love what you said about seeing thoughts on a piece of paper," Melissa told me. "That really helped. When I think about it that way, it becomes a lot more realistic for me to try to meditate." I still consider myself a meditation student rather than a teacher, but in that moment I felt as if I was passing on this sacred piece of knowledge that many meditation teachers have shared with me.

*practice*  ## Quiet Stillness Ritual

When I began to meditate, I found it less intimidating to think of myself as being still and silent rather than *meditating*. Here are some suggestions for creating your own quiet stillness ritual. It has become one of my most treasured daily anchors that helps me become more aware of how I'm feeling and what I'm thinking:

**Find a quiet spot where you can be undisturbed for a few minutes.** Ideally, you can return to this space daily. Over time, when you come to this space your mind and body will get a cue, a reminder that this is time to be still and silent.

**Make your stillness spot comfortable.** I put a few cushions on the floor of a small room in our basement. Maybe yours is a comfortable chair, some blankets on the floor, a couch, or your bed.

**Set a timer.** By knowing that something else is keeping track of the time, you're releasing your brain from that task and giving it an opportunity to drop into quiet stillness. It's up to you how long you want to be still and silent, but I suggest starting with just a couple of minutes. Increase the time as you find it comfortable.

**Create a "start" cue.** Mark the start of your ritual with something simple. You can take three deep breaths. Or light a candle. Or both. But find a way to begin that you can repeat every time. Repetition will help you drop into the still and quiet space faster and easier over time.

**Just breathe.** Don't try to do anything other than sit quietly and breathe. If your mind is very distracted, that is okay, but you may find it useful to repeat a simple mantra, which can be nothing more than "I breathe in, I breathe out," or "I am" ("I" on the inhale, "am" on the exhale).

**Practice awareness.** As you become aware of your thoughts, practice observing them rather than reacting to them. You might find it useful to visualize your thoughts as being typed on a piece of paper, which helps create a bit of distance between you and them.

**Create an "end" cue.** When the timer goes off, don't just jump up and run away into your day. Do something simple to signal the end of your ritual. Take three breaths again, smile to yourself, check in with how you're feeling, or set an intention to be a little less reactive as you go through your day.

There is great power in practicing our ability to recognize that we're *not* the thoughts in our mind or the voice in our heads—we're the ones who hear it. We can take a step back, find the place of the observer, and witness what the voice is saying, as if observing someone else. This puts us back in the position of choice. This sounds simple, but for me this was a profound realization, one that I owe to the ever-wise Michael Singer, author of *The Surrender Experiment* and *The Untethered Soul*. I can honestly say that it's been one of the most important steps on my emotional and spiritual journey.

So who hears the voice in your head?

The one who hears the voice in your head is your inner witness, the deeper and wiser part of you. This is what Janet meant when she talked about my *true self* or *higher self*. This is what Michael Singer means when he says that you, the real you, is the one who is aware of your thoughts and the voice in your head.

This was a difficult idea for me to grasp for a while: Was there some other person inside listening to my thoughts? But I came to realize that it's not a different person at all, but rather a different part of me that I can learn to connect to, the part that witnesses more than judges.

I like to think of my inner witness as an awesome grandparent who is patient and compassionate, deeply rooted in life experiences, and not easily thrown into fits of anger or overwhelm. In contrast, the voice in my head is more like a child who runs from one place to another, unable to hold attention in one spot for more than a few seconds, going from feeling peaceful one instant to completely freaking out and throwing a tantrum in the next.

When I first became aware of the sometimes crazy and cruel voice in my head, my instinct was to try to shut it up. I literally tried to yell, "Shut up!" But that doesn't really work. (If you have ever tried to calm a child who is in the middle of a tantrum by screaming at them, you know just how pointless that is.) Instead, the practice of acceptance asks that we connect to our inner witness, our inner grandparent, and treat the frazzled, crazy, or having-a-tantrum voice with awareness. When a child is freaking out, a kind and wise grandparent remains steady and compassionate, sometimes giving the child some space to get the negative energy out, sometimes gently drawing them into a conversation that helps the child calm down. The very act of acknowledging the upset child in our mind from a place of awareness rather than anger or annoyance helps calm them down, even if just a bit. Earlier we talked about research showing that acknowledging difficult emotions helps reduce their intensity and duration—this is the real-life application of that research.

Most importantly, the grandparent *chooses* how to react. They don't just follow the child mindlessly deeper into the tantrum. This is the core of our practice once we become aware of the voice in our head: to make a conscious choice about how we want to react to it. My friend Patricia Karpas, a longtime mindfulness and meditation practitioner and the host of the *Untangled* podcast, has a wonderful perspective on how cultivating her inner witness through meditation benefits her: "Mindfulness practice gives me the spaciousness with which to make a choice of how to react to what I feel," she said. "In that space, in that pause, I have a moment of inquiry into what I am feeling, and I can shift from being on autopilot to choosing how to react."

Alison Wood Brooks, a professor at Harvard Business School, conducted a series of fascinating studies that show just how useful the practice of cultivating our inner witness can be for dealing with emotions such as anxiety. She asked study participants to perform activities that most people find anxiety inducing: sing "Don't Stop Believin'" by the band Journey in front of the group of people, deliver a two-minute public talk, and solve several math problems. Before they did anything, some participants were told to say to themselves "I'm excited," some were told to say "I'm calm," and some to say nothing at all.

The "excited" participants sang better according to measurements of their volume and pitch. They spoke longer during their talk and were viewed as more persuasive and confident. They also did better on their math test than other groups. What happened? Anxiety and excitement are similar emotions physiologically: your heart beats faster, your cortisol rises, and your body gets ready to jump into action in response to both emotions. This study showed that by giving your mind more context for *why* your body is feeling this way, you can reframe your anxiety as excitement and improve how you perform in a situation that is making you anxious.

I love this study because it reaffirms how becoming aware of how we feel and reframing the voice in our head can help us better deal with challenging situations. In fact, it confirms why meditation helps reduce stress. Even a short mindfulness meditation practice, during which you simply sit still and focus on your breath, helps calm the amygdala, the part of the brain that is activated during anxiety, fear, and stress. By calming the amygdala, meditation helps us shift out of the fight-or-flight mode of reacting to what we feel and instead make more conscious choices rooted in awareness.

You don't have to meditate to gain the benefits of acceptance—although I encourage you to give it a try because learning to observe your thoughts while sitting on a meditation cushion trains you to do it better as you go through your daily life. When you shift from immediately reacting to unavoidable reality to witnessing it more neutrally, you create an opportunity for yourself to *choose* your path forward rather than spin out. And when you give yourself permission to experience the feelings that emerge in response to any situation, as difficult as they may be, you boost your emotional immune system and enlist it as your ally to help you move along your path with more resilience and perhaps even a few more moments of peace or joy.

## Your Daily Anchors Check-In

Take a moment to consider whether you might want to make any of the practices in this chapter one of your daily anchors. If you didn't get a chance to practice them yet, no problem—just go back now and give them a shot. If you're looking for somewhere to start, begin with the Quiet Stillness Ritual. Remember to give yourself a bit of time with each new daily anchor to see how it makes you feel. A week is a good time frame to start with.

# 7

# Gratitude

There are only two ways to live your life.
One is as though nothing is a miracle.
The other is as though everything is a miracle.
ALBERT EINSTEIN

One of the benefits of acceptance is that it allows us to more clearly witness our reality as it is and, with a bit of practice, find moments of joy or meaning even if things aren't so wonderful overall. A while ago I received this email from Linda, a member of the Happier community, in response to a message I had written about finding some relief from a debilitating headache by focusing on small moments I was grateful for. Linda wrote about her experience with something much scarier—cancer—and the surprising strength she found to face her circumstances:

In July 2001 I was diagnosed with breast cancer. I had just turned forty and my very first mammogram showed cancer cells. At the time I was a single parent to my then seven-year-old little girl. It was an especially difficult time because my daughter's father and I were estranged and he lived across the country from me. My family was in denial and they weren't very supportive of me during surgery or my radiation treatment.

I had a lot of fear and sadness about not being able to earn a living or worse, leaving my daughter without a mother. As the weeks after surgery passed, my sadness turned into severe depression. I was exhausted by the treatments and having to drive myself sixty miles round-trip to receive them and drained by having to take care of my daughter's needs. On top of this, I felt so much stress from worrying about money. I was only making 60 percent of my regular income on short-term disability.

My depression got so bad that I sought out a family therapist. During one of my therapy sessions, I was feeling especially down. My wonderful therapist told me that humans are like chickens: we see worms and then, like chickens, pull them out from the ground. I was pulling out the worms of feeling sorry for myself, feeling abandoned, feeling alone. I felt justified but my downheartedness was only making me feel sadder. So she asked me to pull out the good worms, to tell her something that was good in my life. It was a hard question to answer, but I said, "Well, I am grateful that I survived cancer—many women do not. I am grateful that my daughter still has her mother—many daughters lose their mothers to cancer. I am grateful that I had health insurance to cover my surgery and my radiation—many people don't have health insurance. I am grateful that the cancer was found in its earliest stages—many find their cancer too late. I am grateful that I have a job to go back to—many people don't have a job to return to after taking a few months off from work.

I was going through all the things that were good in my life and that I was grateful for and I realized that I HAD NEVER DONE THAT up until that moment. That day changed my life forever!

With God's blessing, I have been cancer-free since 2001. After that valuable and life-changing lesson in my therapist's office, I learned to find the joy and many blessings, even in the darkest of days. Later on I even found myself grateful for HAVING BREAST CANCER. It taught me to be grateful for every day and never take anything for granted.

So now whenever I have an especially difficult day, I focus on what I am grateful for. When I get a bad headache, for example, I list all the things I am grateful for in that moment: I am grateful that my body is talking to me—it's telling me to slow down. I am grateful that I can work from home so that I can rest in my bedroom to recover from my headache, whereas many people have to continue to work, even with a migraine. I am grateful that it's only a bad headache—and not something more serious.

Linda's story stayed with me for months after she wrote in. What incredible courage! She had every reason to feel sad, overwhelmed, and scared. Not only did she accept her situation, but she focused her attention on what she could appreciate in her circumstances and feel a genuine gratitude for. In an unexpected way, getting cancer had made her happier because going through something so traumatic taught her to appreciate many more aspects of her life. That, in turn, helped her persevere through such a challenging experience.

When something terrible happens, finding even a few things we appreciate contributes to our resilience. It reminds us that our life is richer and broader than the current crisis we're facing. Remember the story I shared in the introduction about my dad's decision to go see the beautiful Vienna Opera House even while we were living in a refugee settlement? He wasn't denying our reality and challenges; he knew that we hardly had any money or enough food to eat, and he didn't know if we would ever get to the United States. Even so, by choosing to be grateful for being able to visit something beautiful together, he reminded us that despite our temporary challenges, we could still experience joy in our lives. Going to visit the opera house that day didn't change our situation, but I'm certain that for my parents, the few hours we spent there were not just a relief but fuel to help them persevere. (I was too stubborn to share this relief, as I shared with you. Boy, did it take me a long time to learn that lesson!)

Researchers have demonstrated this link between gratitude and resilience. In his book *Thanks: How Practicing Gratitude Can Make You Happier*, Robert Emmons, a psychologist at the University of California, Davis, offers a powerful example. In 1992, Hurricane Andrew swept through Florida. It was one of the deadliest natural disasters in the state's history. One study found that for parents who lived through the hurricane, one of the main factors that strengthened their resilience in the aftermath was feeling grateful for what they had *not* lost during the disaster. No doubt they went through a horrific experience, but gratitude offered them a way to broaden their emotional lens and feel some optimism and peace. While they lost a lot, they didn't lose everything.

Practicing gratitude amidst challenges has nothing to do with lying to ourselves or cheating on reality (which is what I'd thought that day at the Vienna Opera House and for several decades afterward). It's not about being grateful *for* something being awful but rather making a courageous choice to focus on something good, however small, *within* the awful. Viktor Frankl, one of the most brilliant psychotherapists of the twentieth century, came up with the concept of tragic optimism while living through the horrors of Auschwitz, a Nazi concentration camp. Frankl realized that optimism wasn't about having illusions but rather recognizing that we can choose our attitude in even the most dire circumstances. Sometimes what we have to be grateful for is just that: our ability and freedom to make our own choices. He writes in *Man's Search for Meaning*: "Man *can* preserve a vestige of spiritual freedom, of independence of mind, even in such terrible conditions of psychic and physical stress. We who lived in concentration camps can remember the men who walked through the huts comforting others, giving away their last piece of bread. They may have been few in number, but they offer sufficient proof that everything can be taken from a man but one thing: the last of the human freedoms—to choose one's attitude in any given set of circumstances, to choose one's own way."

Gratitude involves making an active, conscious choice to focus our attention on something positive in our lives, even when things may be very challenging. This doesn't mean that you need to feel good when something bad happens—in fact, if you read the previous chapter you know the value of allowing yourself to feel how you feel, whether it's good or bad. But bringing something you're genuinely grateful for into focus gives you more strength to get through whatever life may bring your way. Gratitude becomes part of the fuel that keeps you going.

*practice* **Creating a Gratitude Ritual**

Consider making gratitude one of your daily anchors. Here are a few suggestions to help you create a simple gratitude ritual:

**Keep it very simple.** One of the reasons we often fail when we try to form a new habit is that we take on too much too fast. Start by committing to practice gratitude once a day.

**Capture it.** While it's helpful to think about something you appreciate, you boost the effects of gratitude if you write it down by hand or as a note on your phone. Our brain tends to ignore some of our thoughts but it's harder for it to overlook something that we write down.

**Get specific.** Writing down something like "I'm grateful that I had a really healthy breakfast this morning" is more effective than "I'm grateful for having food." Specific details will help your brain register your gratitude with more intensity and help you feel more joyful. It's also important to try to think of something new every day, otherwise your brain will get used to your gratitude and stop paying attention.

**Link your gratitude ritual to something you're already doing.** It's a lot easier to stick to doing something new when you connect it to something you already do regularly. For example, you might write down a few things you're grateful for as you brew your coffee or steep your tea in the morning, or right after you brush your teeth at night.

## Magnifying Joy

The beauty of practicing gratitude is that it doesn't only help us persevere through difficult times but also amplifies the good in our lives when things are going okay. Earlier I shared with you several studies that showed how doing something as simple as writing down several things you're grateful for every day leads to increased life satisfaction. Like a magnifying glass, gratitude helps us savor and truly experience the small moments of joy or contentment that are already there—the same moments we might otherwise not notice as we rush through our busy lives and routines.

Researchers, including psychologist Ed Diener, show that the *frequency* of positive experiences has greater impact on how good we feel than the *intensity* of these experiences. In other words, many small moments of joy make us happier than one big exciting experience—as long as we're aware of them. Sometimes this simply requires that we notice what we're doing and remind ourselves to appreciate the experience rather than taking it for granted. Other times it requires that we get creative and infuse our experiences with a bit more beauty or care. Darlene, a member of the Happier community, shared her story with me. It offers a wonderful example of how practicing gratitude during a stressful time not only helped her feel a bit more calm, but also led to a beautiful annual ritual:

> I want to share with you a personal holiday ritual I started twenty years ago. It was my first year back to work after my daughter was born and I was working in a retail store that played a Seattle radio station as background music. There was this piece of instrumental music that would come on every afternoon called "Angel Eyes" by Jim Brickman. I found it so beautiful I decided to order the album. Compact discs had taken over cassette tapes, but my car still had a tape deck so I had to special order the cassette.
>
> It took a while for the cassette to come in and in the meantime, the Christmas chaos had started in the mall. Between the endless Christmas music and noise of the crowds, by the end of the day I could not wait to get home. The day I got the tape I had forgotten all about it until just before I started clearing the dishes from the table and getting my daughter ready for bed. I put the tape in the deck to play and all of a sudden this incredibly beautiful sound filled my senses and I started to cry. I had been so caught up in the pressures of work, Christmas, and family life that I had forgotten to take

a moment every now and then to just breathe. Here was this beautiful sound and I almost let it become background noise.

The expression "sometimes you must stop and smell the roses" just smacked me right in the eardrum. Needless to say, I stopped what I was doing, gathered up my little girl, and sat down on the couch to listen to the entire album. Every year now I purchase a new piece of instrumental music, and when the holiday madness gets a bit much, I stop and hear the roses.

When we pause to savor some of the sweet moments within our daily routines, our lives become much more enjoyable. It's so simple. It doesn't ask that we do more, run faster, or try harder. We simply have to pause long enough to notice. It could be a moment of beauty or comfort, the good taste of our food, the notes in a piece of music, a patch of sunshine that greets us as we head out for the day. Like Darlene, we can experience more joy in our everyday moments by shifting the question from *How much can I get done during this busy time?* to *How can I get this all done and savor some moments at the same time?*

*practice*

## Savor It

Make a conscious effort to savor something. It can be something you eat, see, smell, touch, or hear. Begin by taking a deep breath and focusing your attention on what you're doing. Allow yourself to simply be in the moment. Do not multitask. As you eat, watch, or listen, pay attention to all the senses: What do you feel? See? Taste? Smell? Hear? Think of this as taking a mental photo of this moment. Finally, when you're done, feel a sense of gratitude for having experienced it, including toward people who made it possible, even if you don't know them. (For example, the farmer who grew the piece of fruit you just enjoyed or the truck driver who delivered the fruit to the store where you bought it.)

## Overcoming Your Natural Negativity Bias

The benefits of gratitude are many: it boosts our emotional immune system and gives us strength to get through difficult times; it amplifies the good and fills us with more joy when things are going okay; and as research I shared suggests, it even improves our physical health. But in order to experience these benefits, we need to make gratitude a regular practice. This is key. The truth is that we're more attracted to the negative, the stressful, and the difficult, which can be really frustrating. This tendency toward the negative isn't a built-in self-defeating mechanism. Rather, researchers suggest that this quality developed to help protect us from potential threats in our environment.

Danger usually involves negative stimuli, so our brains are constantly scanning our environment for something that's wrong, often ignoring positive experiences in the process. I frequently hear people say that they're upset with themselves for being so negative, for always noticing what's wrong or what needs to be fixed. I tell them the same thing I tell myself whenever my negativity bias goes into overdrive: It's not your fault and you're not doing anything wrong. It's the brain doing what it thinks is right and trying to make sure you stay safe and protected. Rick Hanson, a professor at the University of California, Berkeley, writes on his blog that our brain is like "Velcro for negative experiences but Teflon for positive ones." He points out that that our amygdala—the oldest part of the brain that regulates emotions and survival functions—uses about two-thirds of its neurons to detect negative experiences and feelings. Ouch.

Not only are our brains naturally drawn toward focusing on and highlighting negative experiences, but negative experiences also have a greater impact on how we feel than positive ones. We're simply more sensitive to them. Researchers such as

Daniel Kahneman, a Nobel Prize winner in economics, have found that we believe that negative stimuli contain more information and value for our survival, and because of that we tend to instinctively give them more weight when making our decisions. This makes sense: eating a poisonous mushroom could kill us while a regular mushroom will just taste good. So of course we spend more time and attention looking for signs that the "mushrooms" in our lives might be poisonous and less time appreciating the ones that aren't.

In *The Upward Spiral*, neuroscientist Alex Korb recounts a fascinating experiment conducted by researchers in Switzerland: "The researchers played recordings of angry or calm voices for subjects to hear. But interestingly, they played the voices at the same time: one in the left ear and one in the right ear. They asked subjects to pay attention to only their left ear or only their right ear. The researchers found that the amygdala responded to the angry voice *whether or not the person was paying attention to it* [emphasis mine]."

This experiment demonstrates that our brain's more sensitive response to negative emotions is automatic; it's not something we can control. This is fundamental to our negativity bias (and yes, kind of a bummer).

But there is good news. We have the ability to *choose* where we focus our attention, and which events, experiences, and memories get our awareness. This is the essence of the practice of gratitude. Gratitude, like acceptance, helps us avoid being pulled into whatever direction our brains naturally want to take us, and instead allows us to make *deliberate* decisions about where to focus. This is truly empowering.

### Gratitude Antidote

Think of something that frequently stresses you out, something you encounter regularly in the course of your days. It can be something simple, like a car honking or someone bumping into you on the subway. Every time that happens, think of it as a built-in reminder to focus your attention on something you appreciate.

By practicing the gratitude antidote, you're doing two awesome things at once. You're creating a cue that reminds you to practice gratitude—which will help you practice regularly—and you're using gratitude to help your brain sidestep its natural tendency to be negative.

To counter our brain's natural negativity bias we must become intentional and disciplined about practicing gratitude. In *Positivity: Top-Notch Research Reveals the Upward Spiral That Will Change Your Life*, Barbara L. Fredrickson, a psychology professor at the University of North Carolina at Chapel Hill, suggests that to truly flourish we need to aim for a positivity ratio of three to one. "This means that for every heart-wrenching negative emotional experience you endure, you experience at least three heartfelt positive emotional experiences that uplift you," she writes.

We originally built the Happier app with the three-to-one ratio in mind. There are many little ways in which Happier encourages users to capture at least *three* moments of gratitude every day. (I don't want to give it all away, but digital confetti and hot air balloons are involved.) In fact, the original corporate name for Happier was Good Times Three, our homage to the idea that we need to balance our difficult, stressful, sad, or frustrating experiences with more uplifting, content, and joyful ones. (As a side note, there is a lot of debate in the research community about what the perfect ratio is. So think of three to one as a helpful rule of thumb of what it takes to course correct our brains that are so attracted to the negative.)

As Dr. Fredrickson points out, practicing the three-to-one positivity ratio allows us enough room to experience a wide variety of emotions without feeling as if we have to avoid certain ones entirely. Earlier I mentioned a study that showed how Vietnam War veterans with high levels of gratitude were more resilient and less affected by post-traumatic stress disorder. They still experienced PTSD, but they had access to many other emotions as well, including positive ones. Gratitude practices aren't bandages to cover up what we don't want to feel, but rather they give us the emotional strength to persevere through difficulties, large and small, and help us amplify the good moments.

In fact, practicing gratitude is even more important when you're feeling down. Research shows that negativity begets more negativity. When you're in a bad mood, stressed, or sad, your brain is even more sensitive to anything negative than it is under normal circumstances. Think about this simple example: You had a great day at work, finished a huge project, got great feedback from your boss, and an awesome thank-you email from one of your customers telling you how your work helped them solve a problem. That is a really great day, right? But as you drive home, someone cuts you off. You feel annoyed. Then you hit unexpectedly bad traffic, which makes you even more frustrated. And then you realize you left your phone at the office—the final blow—and suddenly you're sure that the universe is out to punish you. In less than half an hour you have forgotten all about your great day at work. Your brain has grabbed onto the small annoyances and amplified them into major frustration that now dominates how you feel. When you get home, everything seems to annoy you, from your dog jumping on you with excitement—*Can't I ever come home to some peace and quiet?*—to your partner surprising you with tickets to a movie—*Why doesn't he understand how tired I am after a long day at work?*

Can you relate? Have you had a similar experience when a series of seemingly small annoyances overwhelm everything else that might have happened that day or week, and leave you feeling deflated, frustrated, or annoyed at the people around you? I think we have all been there.

One of my favorite ways out of these negativity spirals is the Gratitude Zoom, which you can do anywhere, anytime. By zooming in on something positive, you take your brain off its negativity bias autopilot and shift it toward something you can appreciate. You turn on gratitude rather than letting your negativity bias rule. I like to think of it almost like one of those barriers that comes down at railroad crossings: we have no choice but to pause when it comes down. Practicing the Gratitude Zoom is like bringing down this mental barrier to shift the direction of your thoughts.

I love this email from Susanna about how she used the Gratitude Zoom to turn around a particularly nasty day:

> I am the primary caregiver for my mom, who is nearly eighty-five years old and has Alzheimer's. I'm also struggling with two kids hitting puberty at once and homeschooling the little hormone-fueled angels at the same time.
>
> This morning my daughter's evil cat left me a huge "present" of barf, and my dog joined in and puked on the bed, which was due to be changed tomorrow morning but guess today was the day! My friend stood me up when I tried to have a coffee date. And the caretaker who is supposed to help my mom is spending all her time on the phone.
>
> ALL OF THIS SUCKS.

But . . . I am now sitting here next to my beautiful mother with an iced Starbucks latte, a cat (not the barfer) on my lap, and a thankful heart that my family is surrounding me. (And the Nashville Predators WON the Western Conference and are going to the Stanley Cup!) Remembering these small things I'm so grateful for was like this amazing ten-minute reprieve!

*practice*

## Gratitude Zoom

When you're feeling down or caught in a negativity spiral, pause and challenge yourself to find something you can appreciate within your experience, however small. For example, if you're sad about being sick and missing out on what you would rather be doing, can you feel grateful that you have medicine or a comfortable place to recover or people around to help care for you?

## The Valley of Joy

In the summer of 2017 I traveled with my family to Tanzania to share some happier skills and practices with the two hundred girls who study at the SEGA (Secondary Education For Girls' Advancement) Girls' School. These girls come from extreme poverty and many of them lost one or both parents to malaria, AIDS, or other diseases. While the school provides them with room and board, in addition to an excellent education, these girls don't have any extras—no toys, phones, jewelry, fun clothes beyond a school uniform, or books other than those in the school library.

Yet they're so deeply grateful for everything they *do* have.

During one of our happier workshops, I asked the girls to write something they were grateful for on huge pieces of paper we had taped around their outdoor cafeteria. Here are just a few examples of what they wrote:

I'm grateful that we have peanut butter at the school.

I'm grateful that I have both of my parents (mother and father!!!).

I'm grateful to have good teachers who care about me.

I'm grateful because I have all my basic needs met at the school!

I'm grateful that we have computers.

I'm grateful because I am alive.

These girls are deeply grateful for the very basic things many of us take for granted. Because they have experienced such intense poverty, safe and clean shelter, three meals a day, and access to an education are special and extraordinary. They're not givens. But most of us don't have the same perspective, and if we do appreciate these "basics," our appreciation happens quickly and fades quickly. Living in refugee settlements with my parents, without much food or certainty about the future, was a difficult experience that I'll never forget. Yet as I sit in the kitchen of my comfortable home in Boston with a fridge full of nutritious food nearby, I catch myself being annoyed that we don't have enough counter space. I wonder how I can be anything but grateful for all that I have today, given where I came from.

I'm less grateful than I could be because my brain has adapted. The blessing and the curse of the human brain is that it's really good at adapting—to the good and the bad. Once it adapts, once we get used to something, we come to expect it to be there. Rather than being in awe of being alive, of having food, water, and shelter, we take these as our rights, as givens, as our baseline, and then we strive for more. This is human and it's completely normal. To survive, we need to quickly learn how to overcome challenges and get used to the changes they bring. But this adaptability also means that we can easily take for granted the good that is already present in our daily lives. That means that we need to fight a bit harder for our moments of joy.

This is exactly what committing to a regular practice of gratitude can help us do—to overcome what I call the curse of the moving baseline (you read about mine in chapter 1). Your moving baseline might go something like this: You feel absolutely, undeniably certain that when you get that promotion, finish a big project, change jobs, lose or gain ten pounds, find your soul mate, move to a different apartment or city, or buy a dishwasher that doesn't make noise when it runs, you'll be happy. You work really hard and the thing you really want happens. You get the promotion. You lose those ten pounds. Your soul mate appears. That new dishwasher makes so little noise you can't tell when it's running. That feels awesome!

But after a short while your brain adapts. Your original baseline catches up to where you are now. The goal that was once something to strive for becomes your new normal, something you expect to be there. You get used to how things are, and you no longer get the jolt of happiness like you did when you first reached your goal. What's worse, because your brain is doing its job of looking for something that is wrong and needs your attention, you begin to notice everything that is wrong with the very thing that you were certain was your path to blissful happiness.

You discover that the promotion comes with new challenging responsibilities. Your satisfaction of finishing a project fizzles when you get another difficult one to tackle. That new job reveals its own stresses and annoyances. You lose ten pounds but find three new things you don't like about your body. Your soul mate turns out to be a real person with flaws rather than the idyllic dreamboat you envisioned. And now that the new dishwasher makes very little noise you notice that the fridge is super loud! The moving baseline is the very reason why our attempts to find genuine happiness through achievements usually fail so miserably.

Here is an email I received from Dylan in the Happier community that so eloquently illustrates how quickly we can adapt to even the most positive changes:

> My family and I had recently inherited a fairly large sum of money during my last year of college. I had grown up middle class, and I worked part-time to help pay for college, while also taking out lots of loans. When we received this money, my mother was not working and my father had just picked up an independent contracting job after being out of work for a while.
>
> Needless to say, that money did increase our happiness—no more daily stressing about money, no more fights about what to spend it on. However, after that initial surge, the good feeling disappeared, and I was left with my same thoughts and patterns, including my negative tendencies.
>
> Money can certainly alleviate stress and make life easier. This is important to mention. But money can't change your bad habits, your negativity, or your moral fiber. That comes from within, and it takes hard work.

The trouble with our adaptability, says Alex Korb, author of *The Upward Spiral*, is that it can dampen our feelings of satisfaction because our expectations determine how happy we feel. When I interviewed him for this book, he told me, "Our happiness depends not on what happens, but on the *difference* between what we expect and what happens." This idea is related to getting stuck in the Valley of Suffering. The minute we expect something to be a certain way—whether it's something amazing, such as being able to fly in an airplane, or small, such as having a good cup of coffee every morning—we rob ourselves of the chance to delight in the fact that *it's better than it could have been.*

In his book, Dr. Korb shares a study about gamblers at a casino. When one group of gamblers was told that the odds of winning were low, even winning a little bit of money made them very happy. But when another group was told that the odds of winning were very high, even when they won more money than the first group, they weren't as happy. Gamblers who didn't expect to win were happier when they won because for them, it was better than it could have been, better than the baseline they had mentally set for themselves.

The space between how our life *is* and how it *could be* if we didn't have some of the things we have come to expect is what I call the Valley of Joy. We *could* live in a world without planes, where trips take months. We *could* live in a world without delicious coffee available to us every morning (I'm a little afraid to even imagine this). But we don't. Incredibly, we don't.

The girls I met at the SEGA School in Africa were some of the most joyful people I'd ever encountered. They're living examples that if we can practice *not* taking even the most basic things for granted, life becomes a series of miracles. We can feel joy in the most mundane moments. The everyday becomes the extraordinary. We get to spend more time in the Valley of Joy.

## Imagine Life Without This

Think of something in your life that you tend to take for granted. It can be as simple as running water or groceries in your fridge, or that you get to listen to music you enjoy or read books that inspire you. Now consider, for a moment, what your life would be like if you didn't have it?

Especially at times when I find myself caught up in thinking about how something is not quite right—flight is delayed, garage door is broken—I remind myself to pause and think: *imagine life without this*. It doesn't mean I don't ever want anything or wish for something to be better, but this simple exercise fills me with deep gratitude for the many amazing things that do fill my life, and it offers a helpful way to prioritize where I spend my emotional energy. Plus, it just feels really good!

## The Power of Giving Thanks

I often think of gratitude as an act of kindness toward myself because it fills my life with joy and strengthens me when things aren't going great. But gratitude can also be an act of kindness that we express toward someone else. As research shows, expressing our appreciation to others may be the most powerful way to experience the benefits of gratitude.

Martin Seligman, one of the most prominent researchers in the field of positive psychology, led what has become one of the most well-known studies showing the benefits of expressing our thanks to others. He and his colleagues tested the impact of five different types of interventions—including writing down what you appreciate about your day—and found that writing a thank-you letter and delivering it to the recipient had the greatest positive impact on people's happiness one month after the study. Researchers highlighted that people who delivered the letter in person and read it out loud reaped the most benefits.

Are you nodding as you read this? I was when I first encountered the study. Of course it feels good to say thank you to someone we appreciate! Yet many people tell me that they had no idea that a tiny thing such as writing an appreciative letter or email could make them feel so good, or that it could be the thing that makes that other person's day. As we have talked about, our tendency is to dismiss simple things as not being meaningful enough to notice or engage in. But expressing genuine thanks is powerful because it reminds us that we have people in our life who care about us. They help us feel less alone in the battles we face, whether they're big or small.

What's more, expressing our thanks can improve the quality of our relationships. In one study, published in *Psychological Science*, participants were asked to do one of four things: express gratitude to a friend, just think about reasons they were grateful to their friend, talk to their friend about something unrelated, or think about neutral topics. When participants expressed their appreciation, they began to see the relationship as one in which they and their friend supported each other. The authors of the study refer to this as "communal strength," and they found that expressing gratitude regularly and frequently enhances the feeling that a relationship is mutually supportive. In another study, Amie Gordon and her colleagues at the University of California, San Francisco, found that people who were grateful for their partners were also more open and responsive to their partner's needs and more committed to their relationships.

It's just too easy to take our relationships for granted, whether they're with friends, family, colleagues, or classmates. We *expect* support from people we're close to; we *expect* them to care about us and to always be around to help out. We often don't pause to appreciate their support and care, and if they don't meet our expectations we leave the Valley of Joy and head right back into the Valley of Suffering.

Whenever I give a talk on gratitude, I ask audience members to do the following exercise. It only takes a minute or two, and it turns out to be one of everyone's favorite things from the talk because it's so simple and yet so powerful. Take a time-out right now to do it with me.

*practice*

## I Appreciate You

Think of someone you appreciate, someone without whom your life would be less fun or warm or fulfilling. Someone whose support is important to you. It might be a family member, a colleague, a friend, or someone else.

Now take out your phone and send them a message, telling that person that you appreciate them and expressing why. The *why* is really important, so please be specific. They need to know what you value in them because they themselves might not fully realize that they're important to you or how they support you.

You don't have to write a long message; one to two sentences is great. Put this book down for a few minutes and do it right now.

Expressing our thanks to someone is such a simple gesture, yet it can dramatically improve how we feel. It's the fastest way I know to get out of my head and shift my energy to feel more uplifted. But what makes this gesture even more magical is that while it brightens up our world, it also warms someone else's heart. Who doesn't want to be reminded that they're meaningful? This tiny act of kindness often brings with it more happiness than we anticipate—both for the recipient and ourselves.

## Your Daily Anchors Check-In

Which practice in this chapter had the most impact on you? Which one would you like to add to your daily anchors? If you didn't get to all of them, take a moment each day to try a new gratitude practice. Enjoy them!

# 8

# Intentional Kindness

The true benefit of kindness is being kind.
Perhaps more than any other factor, kindness gives meaning
and value to our life, raises us above our troubles and our
battles, and makes us feel good about ourselves.
PIERO FERRUCCI

Can you remember a time when a very small act of kindness—something you did or that someone did for you—filled you with warmth or brightened up a rough day? I've asked this question of many people and it always amazes me how many of us are touched by the smallest gestures that we often remember for years afterward.

A few months ago I received an email from Jen, a member of the Happier community, who shared an experience that really brought this to life. It happened when she was taking her ailing husband to the movies:

> My late husband had ALS. Near the end of his life, when he was a quadriplegic and on a ventilator, it was hard to get out of the house and get around on our own. It was hard to navigate a world that wasn't always accessible to us. It sometimes felt overwhelming.
>
> Once, we were leaving a movie theater. I was operating the wheelchair and carrying the suction machine, while the

back-up emergency bag hung on the back of the chair. As I approached the manual push doors, I slowed down and got ready to turn around and use my back to push them open—not graceful and not that effective either. Then a girl, maybe eleven or twelve years old, walked over and quietly pushed the doors open and held them open for us.

It's been at least seven years since that trip to the cinema. I couldn't tell you what movie we saw that day, but I have never forgotten the warmth that spread through my soul when this young girl came out of nowhere and silently held the doors open like an angel.

This tiny act of kindness made a lasting impression on Jen. To hold the door open for someone seems almost like an afterthought, the simplest thing anyone could do. Yet like many other small acts of kindness, it made Jen and her husband feel significant and cared for at a moment when they were feeling vulnerable. It helped her feel as if she wasn't alone. It was so meaningful that this tiny encounter stayed with her long afterward.

## The Necessity of Human Connection

Most of us want to be connected, included, cared for, and supported. This is why tiny acts of kindness, from people we know as well as from strangers, touch us so deeply. They remind us that someone cares enough to *see* us, to be aware of our presence, and to reach out. Every time we do something kind or are the recipients of kindness, another strand in the fabric of human connection gets woven into our lives. Not only does this bring a moment of warmth and, often, joy, but we're also reminded that we're not moving through life alone—and that can be an invaluable source of strength for us when we go through difficult times.

One day in physics class, during my first year of school in America, a girl named Kiara pushed her notebook closer to me so I could see her notes. She saw me struggling to understand what the teacher was saying and thought that her written notes might help me. They did. But what mattered more—and why I still remember that moment so clearly almost thirty years later—is that she *noticed* that I was struggling and wanted to help me. In retrospect, I recognize that so much of the fear and sadness I felt during those first few years after we immigrated resulted from not having many positive human interactions. I often felt very alone. Kiara's gesture was a small reminder that someone cared, wanted to help, and thought I was worthy of their attention.

The feeling of belonging is at the very core of our needs as human beings. The psychologist Abraham Maslow proposed five different kinds of human needs that motivate our behavior. This theory, first developed in 1943, became known as Maslow's hierarchy of needs, and it has been reaffirmed by many psychologists since. According to Maslow, after our most basic needs for survival are met through adequate food, shelter, and safety, we need to feel like we belong. Without regular social interactions, we feel lonely and isolated, and as a result our health can suffer. A growing number of studies show that feeling isolated can interfere with our sleep and increase our stress, risk of depression, and chances of having a heart attack or stroke. In fact, social isolation is considered by many experts to be one of the most serious health hazards we're facing in our modern society, as dangerous as smoking. In one startling study, Andrew Steptoe, a professor of public health at the University College, London, followed 6,500 people, all over the age of fifty, for two years. Those who were most socially isolated—who had the least contact with family and friends, and didn't participate in community groups or organizations—were 26 percent more likely to die during the study period than those with the most active social lives. (Researchers controlled for factors such as age and illness.)

Having trusted and supportive relationships isn't just essential for our physical health but also for our emotional well-being. In the Grant Study, a seventy-five-year-long study that followed several hundred male Harvard University students who graduated between 1939 and 1944, researchers at Harvard Medical School discovered that there was *one* key factor that the happiest men in the group had in common. The researchers knew the men's family histories and assessed their physical and emotional well-being at regular intervals from 1939 onward. They also ran a parallel study of disadvantaged men in Boston's poorer neighborhoods for comparison. Many of the original study participants went on to have extremely successful lives—President John F. Kennedy was one of them. When asked about the factors that made some participants happier and healthier than others, the researchers had an unequivocal answer: the strength of their close relationships.

"Warmth of relationships throughout life has the greatest positive impact on 'life satisfaction,'" wrote George E. Vaillant as a part of the study's conclusion. "Happiness is love. Full stop."

Not money. Not career success. Not where they lived or how often they exercised. The warmth of these men's relationships, with their parents and with their spouses—their closest people—is what separated the happier and healthier study participants from the others. (Yes, I wish they had included women in the study, but other researchers have demonstrated that women benefit from strong relationships in similar ways.)

As soon as I read about the Grant Study, I texted and called many of my family members and friends just to check in and tell them I was thinking of them. One of my friends replied, asking if I was okay. My text to her said something simple, like "Just want you to know how much I love you."

Her worried reaction was another wake-up call: We often reserve our expressions of kindness for special occasions or times when we or people we care about are facing pain or tragedy. Yet doing something kind intentionally and regularly—without waiting for a special or difficult occasion—is one of the easiest ways to strengthen our relationships with people we love.

*practice*

## Check In

Once a day, perhaps in the morning or before you go to bed, think of one person you care about and check in on them. It can be as simple as sending a message to ask how they're doing or to say that you're thinking of them. If you're near the person—perhaps you live with them—you can do this the low-tech way, face-to-face. You'd be amazed how great this tiny act of kindness makes them feel and how much joy you experience as you do it. Make it a habit!

## Cultivating Kindness in Close Relationships

We might assume that people we're close to already know how we feel about them—that we value and appreciate them—so we don't tell them often enough. We don't put small acts of kindness toward them at the top of our list. But think about how enlivening it feels when a family member or friend tells you something good about yourself. It makes you feel great, and it makes you feel good about them too.

A few years ago I had a chance to spend the day with Deepak Chopra. Together, we had created several courses for our Happier community and we were shooting videos to include in them. One of the questions I asked him was if he had any advice for the quickest way to feel happier right now. He replied, "If you want to feel happier, right this very minute, make a friend smile. The best way to do this is to think of something good they've done or something great about them, acknowledge it and share it with them. It can be a simple text message, but if you make it authentic, it will make them happier and you'll feel amazing."

This sounds so normal and easy. But what's hard about this is that most of the time, our brain's negativity bias makes us very quick to point out what's lacking in our close relationships, or what we want these people to do differently. Barbara L. Fredrickson, the psychologist who came up with the three-to-one ratio of positive thoughts to negative thoughts, suggests that successful relationships—including marriages—need a *five-to-one* ratio of positive to negative interactions. Not all researchers agree with Fredrickson's exact math, because it's hard to be so precise when it comes to human emotions. But even so, she makes a valid point. It's hard to overdo the positive gestures when it comes to our closest people.

My teacher, Janet, suggested that as part of my spiritual work I try to do small kind things for my husband, Avi. I protested. *Why should I be kind first!* In my head I had a very long list of ways that Avi had hurt me over our fifteen-year marriage, and many reasons for why he was wrong and I was right. I had an equally long list of ways I had hurt him and ways in which I was wrong and he was right. Each wrongdoing contributed to the big pile of guilt I was carrying around. It felt as if before I started being kind to him, we should sit down, compare our lists, and tally the wrongs to figure out who had more and who had less. Then the person with more wrongs should be kind first.

"That kind of life math will never work out," Janet said when I shared my hesitation (read: stubborn resistance) with her. "I'm not asking you to be kind *for* Avi, or as a favor to him. I'm asking you to be kind for *you*.

"You experience 100 percent of the feelings you share with others," she continued. "When you feel angry, you experience anger. When you do something kind, you feel kind inside. And *kind* feels better."

I would be lying if I said I was convinced immediately. Avi and I had been together for almost two decades and faced many of the challenges inherent in spending half your life with another person. Somewhere between the usual hectic juggling of regular life stuff and more serious storms we'd faced, both individually and together, the fabric of kindness had thinned out. So it felt strange and scary to do what my teacher asked of me.

But I couldn't get Janet's words out of my mind. I knew I had to try, even with the tiniest of gestures, to be kinder to Avi. It did feel good, but at times I was paralyzed by the fear that my kindness wouldn't come back to me. *What if I'm kind but Avi doesn't reciprocate or notice? What if I make him coffee and he doesn't make one for me? What if I text to ask about his day and he doesn't ask about mine?* I hid behind my fear of opening up and instead pulled back on some kind things I was going to do.

One day Avi and I got into a fight. I stormed off, running an errand to blow off steam. I wasn't being kind; I was indulging my anger. Half an hour later, my phone pinged. "Let's meet at Pavement in half an hour for a latte," Avi texted me. "I'm driving to meet you now."

I had told him under my breath that I was going to the Apple store to fix my phone. Our favorite coffee shop is near that store. I was struck by Avi's reaction to our fight and my anger: he chose kindness. Instead of figuring out who was wrong or who was right, talking ourselves to death trying to do the math and unpack all the unpackable details, we met at the coffee shop, hugged, and shared a latte and a nice walk.

As simple as Avi's gesture was, it required courage. To do something kind or compassionate for someone else asks us to be vulnerable, to open up a part of ourselves that we might be reluctant to expose. That can feel really scary. We have to move past the wall that our ego puts up as it yells about relationship math and who did what wrong how often, or tries to convince us that it's more important to be right and angry than kind. This self-protectiveness can be challenging to get around! To be compassionate, we often have to expose a piece of our core humanity, and do it without any guarantee that the other person will do the same in return.

In *The Art of Asking*, Amanda Palmer writes intimately about the fear of asking that most of us experience—for anything: help, money, supplies, a place to sleep. She writes, "And to be sure: when you ask, there's always the possibility of a *no* on the other side of the request. If we don't allow for that *no*, we're not actually asking, we're either begging or demanding. But it's the fear of the *no* that keeps so many of our mouths sewn tightly shut."

There is a connection between asking someone for help and doing something kind for others: our vulnerability. We risk sharing a piece of ourselves: a need, a tenderness, an admission of our humanness. But that risk, that vulnerability, is what makes both the act of asking and being compassionate without expectations so beautifully courageous. Learning to do this even when we're afraid of rejection connects us to the deepest, truest part of ourselves, the part that is full of love, care, and warmth—the core of what it means to be human. As Janet said, by doing something kind we experience kindness, and in that way we're both on the giving and receiving end of our bravery.

So when you're hesitating on the brink of extending your kindness and compassion, remind yourself how a simple, kind gesture helps you tap into the part of you that makes *you* feel good. Be kind because it feels awesome even if you're not sure how the other person might react, or whether they will be kind to you in return.

## Overcoming Obstacles to Kindness

If you find yourself in a situation where you're having trouble being kind to someone, take some time to reflect on the following questions. You might find it helpful to write your thoughts in your journal.

- Why do you feel you're having trouble being kind to this person?
- What are a few things, even if they're really small, that you appreciate about this person you're having a hard time being kind to?
- Can you recall a time when this person did something kind for you? How did it make you feel?
- What good might come from your courage to be kind toward this person?

## Hardwired for Kindness

Being kind to others isn't just a nice idea. Researchers have found that one of the best ways we can cultivate our own physical and mental well-being—literally, our health—is to regularly do something thoughtful or helpful for someone else. In one study, Sonja Lyubomirsky, a professor at the University of California, Riverside, who has studied happiness for more than two decades, looked at how prosocial behavior (doing acts of kindness for others) and self-oriented behavior (doing acts of kindness for oneself) affected participants. Lyubomirsky and her colleagues found that over the course of their six-week experiment, people who did kind things for others experienced greater psychological flourishing, including more positive emotions.

If you have ever volunteered, you know how great it feels to do something to help others. Dozens of studies show that when we volunteer we feel more socially connected, which helps ward off loneliness and depression. This also applies to how we spend money. Michael Norton, a professor at Harvard Business School, has written extensively about using money to improve how you feel. He and his colleagues conducted several studies that show that we're happier when we spend money on others versus when we spend it on ourselves. In one study they found that spending as little as five dollars on another person increased how happy participants felt.

It seems that we're literally hardwired for kindness. When we do something kind, our brain releases oxytocin, a hormone that makes us feel really good. You may have heard it referred to as the "hug hormone," and, in fact, giving or getting a hug does release it. But it may do more than just make us feel warm and fuzzy inside. Studies show that because it dilates blood vessels, oxytocin can lower blood pressure and improve our heart health. This may be one of the reasons why people who have stronger relationships tend to be healthier. We're hardwired to be kind, and that kindness keeps us healthier.

James R. Doty, a neurosurgeon and the author of *Into the Magic Shop: A Neurosurgeon's Quest to Discover the Mysteries of the Brain and the Secrets of the Heart*, talks about the idea that we have evolved to be kind. One of the things that separates us from other mammals is the use of abstract, complex language that requires a larger and more complex brain. To allow time for the brain to develop, we take care of our young longer than any other species. We have evolved to be motivated to do this—meaning, to deal with sleepless nights, diaper changes, tantrums, teenage angst, and so many other challenges. When we engage in nurturing and compassionate acts, our brain's pleasure center is activated and releases oxytocin. Researchers talk about a "helper's high," the awesome feeling we get when we help another person. It just feels good to see someone's life improve, even in the smallest way, because of something we have done. Happiness is contagious, and we'll dive into this a bit later in the book.

After I shared some thoughts about the power of tiny kindness gestures with the Happier community, I received this email from Elaine. She had just put her kindness practice into action during her regular commute between Dallas and New York:

> I'm sitting here on a 737 on the tarmac at LGA airport in NYC. I make the commute from Dallas to NYC and then to Connecticut every week: out here on Monday and back home on Thursday. Every single week. The commute is the hardest part of not only my job but my life.
>
> Right before I opened your email about the power of tiny kindness gestures, I noticed the woman next to me distressed about her younger friend who was sitting in the row diagonal to me. With my "platinum" status I had boarded the plane about twenty minutes earlier and had the coveted window seat; the woman next me was one of the last on the plane. I could tell she was worried. I decided to ask her why.
>
> Turned out her friend was a special needs kid with whom she works. He was TERRIFIED of planes and she was worried about him getting through the flight. In a second I offered to switch seats with him. She gleamed and just kept saying: "God bless, God bless!"

I would be lying if I didn't say that, at first, I was annoyed when this woman and her friend climbed into the plane late, didn't know where to put their bags, etc. I was feeling very entitled about my window seat. But that experience of paying attention, talking to a stranger, and doing something nice for them just made me feel so much happier about the terrible commute I have to do.

Then, bam! I get your email about kindness. If I hadn't read it, I wouldn't have realized that that tiny act of kindness made me so happy!

How many of us have been in Elaine's situation but didn't offer to switch seats? How many of us have sat down on a plane or train and hoped with baited breath that the seat next to us would remain open? I often take the Acela train between Boston and New York and have gotten used to the various maneuvers people make to prevent someone from sitting down next to them. They pile up their stuff on the open seat. They open the newspaper in a way that makes it difficult for someone to sit down. They pretend to be asleep—with one foot across the empty seat. I'm ashamed to admit that a few times when I was taking a late train home after an exhausting day of meetings, I left my bag and coat on the seat next to me, hoping to get the row to myself.

After I read Elaine's email I made a point to keep the seat next to me on the Acela empty and open. You know what's awesome? The look of happy surprise on the person's face when I say, "Yes, it's open—please," and they take the seat. Do you know what is even more awesome? How great this makes me feel, this tiniest possible gesture of kindness and humanity, one that literally takes zero effort and involves very little sacrifice on my part.

What is so inspiring is just how really tiny the acts of kindness can be, and yet they still make us feel amazing—switching seats on a plane, as in Elaine's case, or taking my bag off the seat next to me in my case. Michael Norton ran a study with his colleague Elizabeth Dunn, who teaches at the University of British Columbia, that asked one group of people going into a Starbucks to have a genuine interaction with the cashier, perhaps to smile at them or have a short conversation. Then they asked the other group to be as efficient as possible—just order, pay, and go. Those who exchanged a few words or a smile with the cashier reported being happier than those who didn't.

I can absolutely relate to the findings of this study. During my initial gratitude experiment, I committed to having one small positive interaction with another person and pausing to smile and say thank you to people I encountered at my coffee shop, yoga studio, and other places I frequented. It became a new part of my daily routine. Before then, I valued efficiency above all and a short conversation with a stranger would seem to stand in the way of getting things done. I couldn't believe how dramatically my life shifted, how much richer, warmer, kinder, more human my days began to feel once I began to prioritize small moments of connection over efficiency. Of course, sometimes I'm in a rush and don't have time to stop and chat—but when I do, it feels like a soul hug. That is the best way I can think to describe it.

Just like with gratitude, I had dismissed the idea that a simple moment of kindness shared with a stranger would make any difference in how I felt. When I thought about kindness, it was usually in the context of doing kind things for my family or friends. But what I've discovered is supported by research, that moments of kindness we share with strangers are valuable and important for our well-being and happiness. Jen, whose story I shared at the beginning of the chapter, didn't know the girl who held the door open for her and her wheelchair-bound husband, and they never met again. But it didn't reduce the lasting impact this small act of humanity had on her. The power of human connection is universal—we can experience it even without knowing the other person.

## Kindness Sprinkles

Here are a few ideas for the simplest acts of kindness you can sprinkle throughout your day:

- Be fully present when you greet people. Put down your phone, look them in the eye.
- Say thank you and mean it.
- Pay someone a genuine compliment.
- Acknowledge people you pass by in the course of the day: the janitor in the hallway, the mail carrier, the barista making your coffee at the coffee shop.
- Check in to see how someone is doing.
- Listen when someone is talking and don't interrupt.
- Hold the door for the person behind you.
- Let something go that a person has done to annoy you.

What are some other things that you would like to add?

## Overcoming the Busy Excuse

In a world where there seems to be no lack of harshness, I find a lot of hope in the idea that we're hardwired to be kind. I love that being helpful and thoughtful is at the very core of being human. But if it's so core and takes so little effort, why do we forget to be kind? Why is it something that often drops to the bottom of our priorities? Why don't we call our relatives more, give more hugs to our family members, reach out to friends we haven't talked to in a while, send simple notes of love to people who are the anchors of our lives, hold doors open and smile at people we encounter in the course of our days?

Liz, a member of the Happier community, shared this story of a time when she skipped the opportunity to help someone:

> I'm still haunted by a young man who asked if I had any money to spare as I was going to a restaurant. I said no and hurried off. A waiter at the restaurant said that he had seen the young man ask me as well as a number of other people and no one helped him. When I left after dinner, I went through my purse and found a gift card to Panera, but I didn't find the young man.
>
> I have many regrets about not helping him. I've started praying for the homeless and giving gift cards to those who are in need. It takes the sting away . . . but only a little.

I was impressed by Liz's courage to admit something that most of us have been guilty of at some point: being too busy to be kind. We can become so fixated on getting where we need to go that we miss a chance to be present and do something kind where we are.

Busy is a real thing. Most of us are juggling way too many to-dos. We're not making it up that we often feel overwhelmed. So what can we do to avoid getting caught up in the busyness and make time for kindness?

"I just don't allow myself to say the word *busy*," my friend Hiten told me recently.

Hiten is a successful entrepreneur in Silicon Valley. He usually runs several companies at a time, advises and invests in dozens of start-ups, all while being a loving husband and a dad to two little kids. If you talk to anyone about Hiten, the words *kind* and *helpful* will undoubtedly come up. I asked him how he makes being helpful such a priority, given the number of responsibilities he juggles.

"Everyone is busy. But here is the messed-up thing: If something happened to you that was life threatening or something happened to a family member or dear friend, you wouldn't say you're too busy to deal with it. You would do what you need to do. You would be there; you would take care of it. There are things in life that make you forget that you're busy, so why bother remembering? Kindness only takes a few minutes."

This is so true. In moments of crisis, we don't hesitate to be kind and help. My friend Amy Jo Martin told me that one of the most impactful moments of her life happened on the night of the 2011 earthquake in Japan. Amy Jo built a very successful digital media agency and accumulated a huge Twitter following—more than one million people. When the earthquake hit, many, including Amy Jo, took to Twitter to help spread information about people who were trapped in the rubble so rescue crews could get to them, and to alert people in Hawaii about potential tsunamis.

"So many people were trying to help," Amy Jo told me. "Everyone pitched in. I was up all night, doing what I could. I felt I had a responsibility to do something because many people followed me, so I could distribute information faster."

That night, Amy Jo witnessed how social media can connect people and spread kindness. Their efforts inspired an idea: If so many people chimed in to help during a crisis, why couldn't we do it as part of our regular life? So Amy Jo decided to try something. Whenever she has a few minutes free, she posts a simple message on Twitter and Facebook: "What can I help you with?" I follow Amy Jo and I've often seen people ask specific questions—"Do you know any great website designers?" "I want to start a career in speaking, do you have any advice for me?"—that she then tries to answer. But I've also seen many people reply just to let her know how refreshing it is to see someone offering help without expecting anything in return.

"I've had so many people write to me to say that they don't need anything right now but they feel better knowing there's kindness in the world," Amy Jo told me.

Moments of crisis shake us out of our habits and routines. They jolt us awake. We become so aware of someone's need for help that we immediately prioritize being compassionate. That is the purpose of creating a regular practice of intentional kindness: to make it a priority in our daily life, without waiting for a crisis to do it for us.

*practice*  **Scheduling Kindness**

One way to prioritize doing something intentionally kind, and to manage our tendency to be too busy, is to schedule kindness. This might seem strange at first—we think of kindness as something that should arise within us spontaneously—but scheduling can be very helpful. We schedule meetings, kid pick-ups, trips to the movies—why not kindness?

You can put "Do something small and kind" on your to-do list or pick a time on your calendar and make it a reminder for yourself. You can even schedule the Check In exercise from page 133 earlier in this chapter.

## How to Ease Conflict with Compassion

Almost every time I give a talk about how kindness increases our feeling of connectedness, I hear this comment: "I try to be nice and kind, but how do I deal with people who are just difficult or rude?" The answer is this: with compassion.

Compassion is the thread that connects our humanity to other people's humanity. When we practice it, we don't feel as negatively impacted by others' behavior when it's less than stellar. We become the beneficiaries of compassion because it helps us feel a little less angry, annoyed, or stressed.

Being on the receiving end of rudeness can be deflating and painful. Just as kindness fuels our sense of being connected to others and makes us feel safe, when someone is rude to us, it's like a knife cutting through our safety net. It can sink our hearts and bring a dark cloud into our day. This can interfere with essential parts of our lives and our ability to perform well at work. In a recent study conducted by University of Florida management professor Amir Erez and doctoral student Trevor Foulk, doctors who received a rude comment were found to be worse at diagnosing and treating patients afterward. The researchers hypothesized that rudeness made doctors feel unsafe, which then led them to close in and not communicate as effectively with their teams, causing mistakes and errors. (Here is a scary statistic: the same researchers estimate that out of 250,000 deaths attributable to medical errors every year in the United States, 40 percent are caused by the negative effects of rudeness on medical personnel.)

To answer the question of how to deal with rude people, I created a workshop that has become one of my favorites to facilitate: the Lens of Compassion. I ask for two volunteers from the audience. One plays a rude and difficult colleague and the other plays a coworker who asks a question. After reminding everyone that, of course, everything we're about to hear is made up, I ask the two volunteers to act out their interaction.

I've led this workshop many times, and yet it's always remarkable how similar the fictional interaction goes. Volunteers playing rude colleagues turn their back, interrupt, and snap at their coworker without ever truly listening to the question being asked. We all know the language of rudeness, it seems. After a few minutes, I pause the two volunteers and ask the audience to break up into small teams—we assign these ahead of time—and write a short story about what might have happened in the rude colleague's day to make them act this way. Once they're done, the teams take turns sharing what they wrote.

The stories are hilarious. The teams get very creative in their dramatic descriptions of terrible events and circumstances that traumatized the rude colleague and made them act so horribly. Here is an example: "Her kids barfed all night, the babysitter called in sick, she got into a car accident on the way to the office, and when she settled down at her desk, one of the legs on her chair broke, causing her to fall and spill coffee on the only copy of the presentation she was supposed to deliver to the company's CEO in an hour."

As entertaining as they are, the stories always have a common thread: they suggest that the person was acting so rudely *not* because they're an awful human being but because they're struggling with something in their lives.

Once we have read all the stories I ask everyone how they now think about dealing with a rude or difficult person. Usually participants decide—after some very lively discussion—that the best way is to give the other person the benefit of the doubt, that something they're struggling with is causing them to act rudely or in a difficult way. Kristin Neff, a professor at the University of Texas at Austin and one of the most well-known researchers in the area of compassion, identifies one of compassion's core components as "common humanity." In *Self-Compassion: The Proven Power of Being Kind to Yourself*, she writes, "Compassion involves recognizing our shared human condition, flawed and fragile as it is."

Recognizing that someone rude has anything in common with us can be challenging, for sure. Approaching difficult people from a place of compassion has always been a big obstacle for me. It's also puzzled me. Why? I'm generally a nice person, so why do I struggle with my own frustration or anger when someone is rude, angry, or unpleasant toward me in some way? When I read the word *flawed* in Kristin Neff's sentence above, it was like a lightning bolt of realization: compassion asks that we accept that we're all flawed and imperfect, and for most of my life, I would never, under any circumstances, allow for that to be true. I believed that the point of living was to try to make things perfect, and this included myself. Of course, I never felt that I *was* perfect, and I beat myself up for that endlessly, but that didn't prevent me from thinking that perfection was possible and achievable.

I wasn't brought up in a culture that accepted imperfection. As a country, Russia was always striving for an ideal and perfect communist society (even if it never achieved anything close). As a student, nothing less than perfect would be considered great. Even some of the ways my family members expressed love involved pointing out flaws that can be improved. We laugh now when my grandpa openly announces during dinner that something doesn't taste great. He'll sometimes say that a dish was better last time. Of course he doesn't mean to hurt those who cooked, usually my mom or me. To him, pointing out flaws is an expression of honesty and care, an effort to help the other person improve.

Striving for perfection makes accepting imperfection intellectually and emotionally challenging. I didn't realize until I began my work with Janet just how stubbornly unwilling I was to accept that I couldn't be perfect, no matter how hard I worked. I'm still a newbie when it comes to accepting myself as I am, with all my many flaws, and I'm still very much a student of approaching difficult people through the lens of compassion.

But when I practice, I feel the benefits. Recognizing that someone's behavior is, at least in part, driven by their personal struggles gives us a chance to be less reactive to all the ways, big and small, that people might annoy us, stress us out, or hurt us.

It doesn't mean we don't ever feel the impact of their actions, but compassion gives us a choice about how to react and how much of their negative behavior to allow into our own feelings.

Here is a powerful story that Teri, one of our Happier members, shared with me recently about how viewing others' rude behavior with compassion inspired her to shift how she reacts to it and has led to some surprising outcomes:

One time I was in one of the newsstand stores at LaGuardia Airport. An elderly woman was working at the register and just as she was about to wait on this very impatient man, her supervisor asked her to move to another register. It took her a few minutes to log into the new register and Mr. Impatient became even more so and he reamed her out.

I was so stunned that I just stood there while the cashier looked embarrassed and uncomfortable. The man paid and quickly left, but it really bothered me that I didn't speak up for the cashier. So I vowed that I would never again remain silent when I see someone being treated badly.

At the same time, I've learned to go easier on rude people based on you never know what burden someone is carrying. I've developed a "go-to" phrase for these situations: "I'm going to assume you're having a really bad day, because that is the only reason I can imagine for the way you just spoke to that person." This gives people the benefit of the doubt, while letting them know that their behavior is unacceptable.

Frequently, people admit that they're having a bad day, tell me why (I'm going through a bad divorce, my mother was just diagnosed with cancer) and then they apologize to the person they offended and to me. Sometimes they even thank me for calling them on their bad behavior and allowing them to apologize. In the end, everyone seems to leave the experience feeling better.

Approaching a difficult person from a place of compassion doesn't mean that you condone or approve of their behavior. It simply means that you allow for the possibility that they're struggling with something, just like you have many times in your life. In its purest form, this is an act of kindness—to assume the best about the other person, to recognize the good in them, and to acknowledge that they're struggling with something that is preventing that inner goodness from coming out in this particular situation. And like other acts of kindness we have explored together, it feels good when we do it—we feel a little less annoyed, a little less frustrated, a little more okay.

*practice*

## Lens of Compassion

The next time you're dealing with a difficult person in your life, try using the lens of compassion. Before you react to their behavior, pause. What is something that person might be struggling with? What might have happened to them to make them act this way? Remember that your story about them doesn't have to be true. The purpose of this exercise isn't to excuse bad behavior; it's to reduce the negative impact this behavior has on you. (In some instances, it may also create a safe space for this person to become more aware of their actions, but mostly this exercise is for you, not the other person.)

## Advanced Kindness

Approaching difficult behavior in others from a place of compassion and acknowledging our common flaws and struggles isn't always easy to do. I call this *advanced kindness*, and it asks for more of our commitment and practice. Like so much of what we're exploring together, it's a practice, which means that we don't always get it right and the best we can do is to try again.

Another practice that falls into the advanced kindness category, at least in my own experience and from what I've learned from others, is accepting other people in our lives *as they are*, without trying to change them, improve them, or even help them feel better when they're going through challenging times. In chapter 6, we explored different ways to practice acceptance of our circumstances and our emotions, as well as the benefits of doing this. When we practice acceptance, we struggle less and have more emotional energy to see our reality clearly. From that point of clarity, we can make better decisions about how to move forward. These are the benefits, the gifts that we share with others when we practice accepting them just as they are.

The small town of Geel in Belgium has a unique tradition that embodies this principle of acceptance in a way that shows what we're truly capable of. At its core is genuine kindness. For more than seven hundred years, its residents have taken mentally ill and disabled people into their families as boarders. They almost never use the term *mentally ill* or know the disabled people's clinical history before they take them in. They know these people can't live on their own but don't have family or friends to help. Some of these "special boarders," as they're sometimes called, end up living with their new families for decades.

The hosts of *Invisibilia*, the podcast that shared this story, went to Geel to meet some of the families who have taken in special boarders. One of the families they interviewed revealed that they had a son of their own who suffered from mental illness. Although he tried, he couldn't live at home with his family and ended up moving away to live on his own. Both of his parents loved him and had been able to take care of other boarders with mental issues. As the mom spoke, you could feel the love in her voice, as well her sadness that she couldn't help her own son.

The podcast episode continued with other stories of people with mental illness being able to function better in communities with strangers versus their own families. In so many cases, the same intense love that the families felt, and the same intense desire they had for the mentally ill people to get better, were the very factors that seemed to make it difficult for them to get better. They felt pressured. They felt as if they weren't doing the right thing. They felt as if their families couldn't accept them just the way they are.

When families who didn't know the mentally ill people took them in, they accepted them and their condition as given. As they cared for them, the families didn't try to change them, which created a safe space for them to just *be*. Because they felt accepted and safe, the boarders could function better and carry out their daily activities. As we explored earlier, the need to feel safe is a fundamental human requirement: we all need to feel safe in order to live our best lives. The story of the people of Geel was a profound reminder of the way that acceptance can help us experience that safety.

As much as we might know that acceptance helps people flourish, it's often difficult to practice. When you love someone, you want them to feel better, be better, reach higher. I wrote to the Happier community about catching myself wishing something else for my daughter—for her to be more organized, more focused, more this, more that. Debbie, a Happier community member, replied. She had been doing the same thing with her son, but by listening to him she found a way to stop herself:

> I needed a wake-up call as to how I was interacting with my son who was twelve at the time and always struggled in school. I was the "queen of buts"—always wanting something more from him. "This is great, but . . ." or "I like this, but . . ." Until one day, while I was talking to him, Steven interrupted me and said, "BUT . . . ?" And you know what? A "but" was coming.

His response stopped me in my tracks. That was my wake-up call!! I said, "No 'but,' Steven," and left it at that. We put so much pressure on the ones we love and expect so much for them and from them. And sometimes we miss the little successes along the way when we're always focusing on the big picture.

Debbie realized that pushing her son this way made him feel inadequate and criticized, which wasn't her intention. She wanted to refocus on acknowledging how he was doing well in the moment, and that he was okay as he was.

The obstacle we often have to overcome on our path toward accepting someone as they are is our own fear. I nag Mia about being organized and more focused because I fear that she won't do as well in school and in life if she isn't. Debbie feared that if she accepted her son's performance in school as it was, then he wouldn't be motivated to do better. To accept someone as they are asks us to practice accepting our own feelings first and then be kind enough to prioritize the other person's well-being above that. I can nag Mia and indulge my own fear, or I can accept my fear—I'm her mom, it's part of my emotional DNA to be concerned for her—and recognize that Mia is more likely to do better in life if I don't spend all my time making her feel bad about not being organized.

This doesn't mean, by the way, that we should never suggest ways that people we care about can improve. In fact, to love someone is to help them become their most beautiful, amazing, best self. But there is a delicate balance there. We can practice becoming more aware of it by asking this question: *Am I making this suggestion (for the person to improve) from a place of my own fear or from a place of true kindness and belief that it will help them?* The answers aren't always obvious, but I've found that pausing to ask this question can bring a lot of clarity about our intentions and help guide our practice of acceptance.

## From Frustration to Advanced Kindness

Think of someone in your life whom you have a hard time accepting as they are. Perhaps it's your child, partner, sibling, or parent. Or maybe it's a friend, classmate, or someone at work. You care about this person but you also find yourself thinking, *I wish she would do this differently*, or, *He is great but it would be better if he would* . . . You might even at times share those thoughts with that person out loud, maybe with some frustration (and by "at times" I mean often, judging by my own experience).

Imagine taking a break from this wishful way of thinking and accepting this person just as they are. Not as an act of giving up on them but as an act of love that helps them feel safe and accepted. To do this, you need to become aware of your wishful thoughts. Practice noticing when those thoughts come into your awareness. You might decide to write them down.

Second, consider why you wish for the person to change. Would this change benefit them, or is your desire driven by your own fear or other feelings? There is no right answer, but spend a few minutes thinking about it.

As the next step, refocus your thoughts on what you appreciate about this person, just as they are. You might also write down their positive qualities to remind yourself. Gratitude will help your brain overcome its natural negativity bias that may be overacting and influencing your wishful thinking.

In my experience, this practice can help strengthen your relationships and allow for more space in which the other person might choose to make those very changes you're wishing for.

One of the most difficult times to practice accepting people just as they are is also perhaps the most important—when they're struggling. A few months ago I had a business meeting scheduled with Erika. A bright-eyed and warm young woman, Erika was already inside the coffee shop when I walked in. During our conversation I told her about my experience of trying to run away from negative emotions, and that I was still learning how to be okay when things weren't okay. I also told her that I'd been trying to do this with my daughter, to both be more honest about not always feeling great and not pressuring her to "get over" negative feelings.

Erika teared up as I talked. Then she told me that a few years ago she was diagnosed with multiple sclerosis. She was twenty-four years old at the time, and one of the more difficult parts of her diagnosis, she said, was how her mom had dealt with it. When she called her mom to share the devastating news, her mom assured her that everything would be okay and then quickly moved on. She told Erika later that she cried after she hung up, but on the phone then and during most of the time since, Erika's mom hasn't allowed any sadness or pain to surface in Erika's presence.

"I'm determined to live a good life, to be successful, to have a family, to do what I need to do to make that happen. But I would have really loved for my mom to give me a little space to be sad, to be sad together with me," she said. "I know she loves me so much, but it's never been okay in our family to be down and not hold it all together."

My heart was aching as I listened to Erika, both because I could feel her pain and could relate to it. We're all seeking permission to feel how we feel, to accept ourselves and to be accepted by people we love both when we feel uplifted and joyful and when we feel sad, afraid, or in pain.

As a parent, I could also understand Erika's mom's desire to focus on moving forward. I could only imagine how much fear she felt for her daughter and how that fear prevented her from expressing any sadness of her own. She might have been afraid she would get stuck in her difficult emotions or disappoint her daughter by being less than positive and upbeat. When someone we love is struggling, we want to help them feel better. This is the very core of what makes us human.

But often that desire pushes us to skip what might be the most important step in helping them: pausing to acknowledge their pain, help them feel less alone in their struggle, and know that we're with them no matter what happens. To do this, we again must face our own fears about how this person is feeling, about their pain and struggles, which is so difficult to do. But if we practice accepting our own emotions and then create a sacred space in which the person we care about feels safe and supported, we may help them be more resilient as they face their battles.

To be compassionate toward others, we first have to acknowledge their suffering or pain in a nonjudgmental way. In *Mindful Compassion*, Paul Gilbert and Choden write that "compassion is the capacity to be open to the reality of suffering and to aspire to its healing." The key here is to be open to the reality first, and then move toward healing.

## Your Daily Anchors Check-In

Is there a kindness practice you want to add to your daily anchors? If you haven't yet tried all of them, give yourself some time to explore. If you have been doing your daily anchors for a week or more, you might consider reflecting on your experience in your journal. Do you notice a difference, however slight, on days when you stick to your daily anchors practice? How do you feel? What's working for you? What doesn't feel quite right? What might you want to experiment with further?

# 9

# The Bigger *Why*

The meaning of life is to find your gift.
The purpose of life is to give it away.
PABLO PICASSO

My dear friend Daphne and her daughter, Gabrielle, stayed at our house just after Gabrielle had graduated from medical school and begun her residency. Over pizza and wine, we talked about the pressure, stress, and exhaustion that residents endure, especially in their first year.

"It's brutal," Gabrielle said. "We work six days a week, with double shifts on many days, which can mean working sixteen hours straight. And there really isn't enough time to release the stress we gather during the day, including the stress from seeing patients and families in pain. But I'm grateful that my work has a lot of meaning and is something I'm passionate about."

She told us a story about a patient she'd recently met who was complaining of horrible sharp pains all over her body. She wasn't responding to various treatments the doctors had been trying.

"Check her thighs," Gabrielle said, remembering that in some cases blood gathering in the thigh can lead to the symptoms this patient was experiencing.

She turned out to be right. The doctors were able to alleviate the woman's symptoms over the next few days. As Gabrielle told the story, her entire face lit up with joy and satisfaction. "That was one of the most meaningful moments of my entire life!"

## The Bridge of Resilience

Having a sense of the greater purpose of our efforts, what I call the bigger *why*, sustains and inspires us when things are good and can be a powerful source of motivation to keep going, even if we encounter obstacles. I'm so energized when I hear from people who say that my work—whether Happier workshops or something I wrote—made a positive impact in their lives. It makes me want to do more and do it better, so I can help more people. When I say that knowing I'm making a positive impact is a huge gift, I mean it quite literally—it not only feels amazing but also fuels me with the encouragement to keep doing my work.

Having a sense of meaning can be uniquely helpful when we need to get through times when not everything is okay. We're all going to have those, no matter what we do in our lives. The bigger why connects us to something more significant than our current difficulties and helps us stay the course when circumstances are less than ideal. When we have a strong feeling that we're doing something meaningful, it gives us resilience. We know that whatever stressful situation we're in right now is part of our journey to serve our purpose, and this helps us accept it and work through it.

This is the kind of reframing that Gabrielle was doing when she told us that the schedule and stress of her residency were brutal but she found a lot of meaning in what she did. She wasn't just stressed; she was stressed as she did something that was helping others.

I'm certain that knowing her bigger why didn't necessarily make her love working sixteen-hour shifts—I don't think that is possible. But she was able to cope better because rather than struggling with her stress, Gabby accepted it as a necessary ingredient of doing what gives her meaning. Her stress had a purpose. As we talked about in the chapter on acceptance, we often spend a great deal of emotional energy feeling upset over having feelings we'd rather not have, such as stress. When she framed her stress as part of something meaningful, Gabby helped herself not waste more energy.

Viktor Frankl, the Austrian psychologist who was interred in a Nazi concentration camp (and who I mentioned in chapter 7), knew that his chances of surviving Auschwitz were very slim. Every day he saw other prisoners either be killed or die from sickness or starvation. There was seemingly no reason for him to keep trying to survive. But he held on to two things: his hope of reuniting with his wife, parents, and brother, who had been taken to different concentration camps, and his desire to publish his book, *The Doctor and the Soul*, which he had written before he was sent to the concentration camp. He had smuggled in the manuscript of this book by sewing it inside his pants, but it was discovered by the Nazis and thrown away. He would spend many nights in the concentration camp, including when he was suffering from typhoid fever, reconstructing the manuscript in his memory so he wouldn't forget it. His love for his family and his desire to share his research with others were his bigger why. It was this sense of purpose that gave him the strength to persevere through unimaginable conditions. (He successfully published *The Doctor and the Soul* after he was freed from Auschwitz.)

In his 1946 book *Man's Search for Meaning*, Viktor Frankl writes, "A man who becomes conscious of the responsibility he bears toward a human being who affectionately waits for him, or to an unfinished work, will never be able to throw away his life. He knows the 'why' for his existence, and will be able to bear almost any 'how.'" If you haven't read this book, run and get a copy—it's incredibly rich with hope, practical ideas, and wisdom just like this, even though it's not always an easy read. (Viktor Frankl's book has sold more than ten million copies and has been called one of the ten most influential books of all time by the Library of Congress.)

Whether we're facing a tragic circumstance, as Viktor Frankl was, or feel stressed in our daily lives, connecting to the meaning of what we do and focusing on our bigger why can help us get through it. In her book *Presence*, Amy Cuddy shares research that shows that people who write down values that are important to them before they enter a stressful, high-pressure situation perform significantly better. They feel more present and connected to their true selves, and so they feel more confident. Our answers to the question "Why?" touch on our core values, on why this is something that is important to us. From that awareness we gain strength to keep going, even if our confidence lags behind.

I love this email from Lynne, a grade-school teacher in Nebraska, who shared how her bigger why helped her relieve some of the stress she was feeling and find renewed energy to continue her work:

> This was a particularly hard school year for me. I teach seventh-grade social studies in Omaha, Nebraska, and at the end of this year I was just done. I have done this for seventeen years and I'd lost my sense of why I do it. When the kids were on the buses and going home on the last day of school, I was ready to just jump into a bottle of wine and my bed. However, I had summer school starting the next Monday so all I got as a break was one day of summer and a weekend.
>
> That night a friend of mine sent me a picture she saw on Snapchat. It was part of a video that said this: "Mrs. Pedersen

is the coolest teacher I've ever known and this summer I'm really going to miss her. Mrs. Pedersen don't change, stay the same." It immediately made me cry. Here I was feeling like I had lost my sense of myself, but this kid wanted me to stay the same. And this happened to be a student to whom I had given a hard time during the year because he was smart but didn't want to do the work.

I felt such a renewed sense of purpose after reading his note and it was such a great way to start summer school. I'm going to hug that kid the next time I see him!

*journal practice*

## Moments of Meaning

What are some times in your life when you felt that you were doing something that was meaningful to you? Write about them in your journal and try not to judge—there are no wrong answers. Also, please don't worry if this is a challenging exercise to do. In the rest of this chapter we're going to explore different ways to help you uncover more meaning in your life, and you can always come back to do this practice later. In fact, I might suggest that it's a great idea to do this a few times a year, as a way to reconnect to your bigger why.

## What It Means to Have Meaning

What does it mean to have a sense of meaning or purpose in life? I think most of us would say that we derive meaning from helping others, whether we do it directly or through our work, a cause we support, or our craft. As we talked about in the previous chapter, we're hardwired to be kind—when we help others we affirm what it means to be human. But there is another element of meaning that is essential: our core strengths.

One of my favorite descriptions of meaning comes from Martin Seligman, the psychologist and author of *Flourish*. Seligman includes meaning as one of five core practices in his model of happiness and psychological well-being, along with positive emotion, engagement and finding flow, relationships, and a sense of achievement (he calls this five-element system PERMA). Here is how he describes having meaning: "When your life is meaningful, you use your highest strengths and talents to belong to and serve something you believe is larger than the self." In other words, meaning is a thread that connects the best of what is within us to something that is outside of us, whether it's our work, our family, a creative pursuit we're passionate about, or a cause we want to support.

According to Seligman, meaning is made up of two parts: (1) meaning taps into our core strengths, natural skills, and virtues; and (2) meaning arises when we share those strengths, skills, and virtues with other people.

In my search for meaning I neglected the first part for a very long time. When I was chasing happiness through overachieving, what I was looking for was more meaning in my life, although I couldn't articulate it that way at the time. I wasn't trying to get great jobs, start companies, and write books just to make money or gain recognition. I wanted to make my parents—and myself—feel as if our struggle to come to the United States was worth it. My love for my family is an important source of meaning for me, and I was trying to do work that was in service to it. I also felt a deep sense of gratitude for having the opportunities that growing up in America provided. It felt purposeful to work really hard to not waste any of them. In a way, these two things became my cause, and the more I worked, created, and achieved, the more I felt a sense of purpose and connection to them.

But what I learned during the years when I began to pause to feel how I actually felt, to become aware of my thoughts and see how many of them came from a place of fear—fear of failing my family or the gift of life in America—was that I had been missing an important component of meaning. I hadn't considered the strengths I already had, the skills and virtues that came naturally to me. I was always rushing to push and out-achieve myself. It was only after I paused long enough to catch my breath that my natural abilities became clearer to me.

Don't get me wrong. I'd had inklings of what these were. Every time I gave talks, no matter if it was to a handful of people or to an auditorium, I felt moments of magic, like I was home, doing exactly what I was meant to do. Whenever I shared a personal experience, with one person or many, to help people learn something about their own lives or paths, I felt I made an impact. I love to write and improve my writing. Every time I shared something I wrote, whether it was a short story or a guide for new interns (something I wrote at one of my internships), it brought joy to people who read it and that felt really awesome.

But I didn't acknowledge these inklings as revealing my core strengths, partly because I wasn't really tuned in to how I felt. I spent much of my time running forward and doing—building and creating—rather than being and feeling. I also ignored them because they didn't fit into my story of who I was and what I was supposed to do. What did speaking, writing, sharing my personal experiences, or coaching small or large groups of people have to do with my career as a businesswoman and entrepreneur? I had created a picture of how I thought my life *should be* and ignored the signs that perhaps I was only serving one part of what brought me meaning.

My teacher, Janet, likes to say that sometimes the universe talks to us through the words of other people. If I look back, the universe was trying to tell me for a very long time to pay attention to my natural skills and strengths. I'd get the message from the mouths of people I knew well or almost not at all. My dad told me for decades, from our first years in America, that I needed to get on stage and speak so I could help more people. I've had strangers come up to me after smaller talks to tell me that speaking is my calling and I should do it more. When I was in my twenties, I sent fifty pages of the story I'd written about our immigration to the United States to an editor at an established New York publisher. Although the story was unsolicited, the editor wrote back to say that my writing was strong and the story, while it needed development, was important to share. (I couldn't invest more time into it because I was working sixteen-hour days as a consultant at McKinsey at the time.) For a year before I decided to write this book and share my personal experiences, I received hundreds of emails from the Happier community telling me that when I shared a part of an experience, no matter how tough it had been for me, it helped them realize something useful about their own lives.

The universe tried to tell me to pay attention to my natural strengths—storytelling, writing, speaking, sharing my experiences in a way that helped others—but I didn't listen until I paused long enough to move from "here is how it should be" to "here is how it *is*." The changes we have made at Happier, including developing our online courses, Happier at Work training, and my becoming much more open about my experiences and what I've learned, come directly from this acknowledgment. This wasn't easy to do because, in the process, I had to relax my own story about who I was (a businesswoman, a tech entrepreneur) and embrace who I had evolved to be (a teacher who was still a student). There was a lot of fear to work through: *What would my business colleagues think of me? Did I have the right to teach others what I was still learning myself? Would I be able to make a living and support my family if I shifted my career this way?*

The beautiful thing about becoming aware of my strengths and finding a meaningful way to share them with the world is that it helped me move through a lot of fear and self-doubt. This is why I call my bigger why one of my daily anchors. It functions as an inner strength I can tap into during moments when my confidence gets shaken up.

I still care very much about my parents' struggles to come to America being worth it and not wasting the gift of building a life here, but I have added another important sense of purpose: helping people live truly happier lives, including learning how to find more joy in everyday moments, and bring compassion to those times when things aren't okay. For the first time in my life I feel that I'm serving these sources of meaning in a way that taps into my strengths and most natural skills. And that feels freaking amazing!

## Identify Your Strengths

As a first step in thinking about what brings you meaning, spend some time writing in your journal about the strengths you already have. What comes to mind when you consider these questions:

- What are you really good at?
- When do you feel most like yourself, truly awake and alive?
- What do people in your life come to you for (support, creative ideas, advice, etc.)?

Don't worry about writing complete sentences, and try not to judge what you write—just get your thoughts down.

If you'd like some ideas to get your thinking going, you can check out the Brief Strengths Test on the website of the Authentic Happiness Institute. Go to authentichappiness.sas.upenn.edu and click on "Questionnaires" to take the test. (You have to register to take the test but it's free.)

As a second step, ask a few people in your life what they think your natural strengths are. This may feel a little weird, but that is okay. In fact, you can tell them that it feels weird to ask. In my experience, most people will be more than happy to share their thoughts with you, especially if they know they can be helpful. You may ask them something like "How do I contribute to your life in a positive way?" Give them time to answer and just listen—you will notice your strengths in their answers. Keep a record in your journal of what they say.

As a third step, spend a few minutes contemplating your strengths, those that you wrote down and the ones your friends or family shared. Which ones really speak to you? Which ones surprised you? (Here is a hint: the things you're great at, that you think are no big deal, may be your most natural strengths. Can you fix anything? Are you an amazing problem solver? Are you the person who can always cheer up a friend who is feeling sad? These are examples of natural strengths.)

Once you identify a few that you relate to, think about how you can practice them more often in your daily life without having to make drastic changes. For example, if one of your strengths is "I'm a good listener," could you find more opportunities to listen to others?

## Discovering Meaning

Where do we look for meaning once we become aware of our strengths? A few years ago, Amy Wrzesniewski, a professor at the Yale School of Management, was curious why some janitors reported much higher job satisfaction than others, even though in most cases they did the same type of work for the same amount of money. She decided to conduct interviews with custodial staff at a hospital.

The interviews started with: "Please tell me what you do in your job." But the answers the two groups of janitors gave were remarkably different. Janitors who reported high job satisfaction spoke about helping patients heal or helping their families feel better while visiting. Janitors who reported low job satisfaction talked about the tasks they had to complete daily, such as scrubbing floors or taking out the trash.

In other words, janitors with high job satisfaction talked about the "why" while those who were less happy at work talked about the "what." Both groups had exactly the same jobs and completed the same tasks every single day on the job. But by viewing their work as a way to help someone else, to contribute to someone other than themselves, the janitors who were attuned to their bigger why *enjoyed* their jobs more. While the researchers didn't talk about this, I believe what helped these janitors was their ability to tap into their strength of empathy and kindness, and from there to find ways to use it to serve other people. They may not have done this consciously, but they had successfully connected the two parts of what gave them meaning: doing something they were good at and contributing to others.

What I found so inspiring about this study is the idea that meaning isn't an inherent feature that comes with some tasks, jobs, or activities, and not with others. Meaning doesn't exist on its own, waiting for us to stumble on it. Meaning is a quality we can infuse into anything we do, including the simplest, most boring tasks, by connecting what we do to serving someone or something other than ourselves, just as the janitors in the research study did.

I recently gave a speech at a team-building conference for a large technology company. Only the top performers were invited, along with their families, and the conference was held in Costa Rica so that participants could also enjoy a few days of rest and relaxation. After I gave my talk to the six hundred salespeople, a tall man approached me.

"I just want to thank you for your talk. You helped me realize something that I never thought about," he said. "My customers are government agencies. Some of them are responsible for keeping our country safe. I never even thought about it this way, but by selling them our software and helping them understand how to implement it to do their work better means that I'm also saving lives. That is really amazing.

"I've worked at this company for many years. I enjoy it. I've done really well financially and have taken care of my family. But today I'm going to go tell my two kids who are here—probably swimming in the pool—that their dad helps save lives by doing his work. I don't think there's anything more meaningful to me than for my kids to know that what I do has a meaning other than just paying for our house or vacations."

This salesperson had unearthed his bigger why—the meaning in his work—at the same job he'd had for more than a decade. He looked so thrilled that it became a meaningful moment for me as well.

One of the most important things I've discovered about meaning is that we don't need to quit our jobs or leave our lives behind to go searching for it. That is an escapist idea for popular novels and fun movies, and I'll admit that I've fantasized about traveling the world to find my sense of purpose, too, especially when I was going through some dark times. It just seems so romantic, doesn't it?

But as I learned and continue to learn, the best way to connect to a sense of purpose is to first look *within* our current lives, within what we already do: in our work, creative pursuits, families, teams, and communities. We can feel a greater sense of meaning once we gain a better understanding of how what we do positively impacts other people.

Several recent studies published in *Harvard Business Review* show that one of the key factors that improves motivation at work is having a direct connection to those who benefit from our work. In one study, researchers found that when colleagues expressed gratitude to each other and shared how another person's work helped them, their engagement with their jobs increased significantly. This resonates a lot. What brings me meaning isn't just speaking or writing but knowing that I'm able to help others through my speaking or writing. The more I connect to that sense of meaning, the more motivated I feel to do even better work. What brought Joy (the woman with spunky hair who came to a talk I gave in New Hampshire) meaning wasn't doing tons of travel and late nights for her work but knowing that her work was helping people live healthier lives.

While these studies were done in the workplace, the findings carry a kernel of truth for all areas of our lives: the most natural place to look for our purpose is in our connections to other people. A great way to begin to uncover more meaning in our lives is to ask ourselves these questions: *How do some of the things I already do help others, and what can I do to amplify the positive effect I have?*

## Meaning Makeover

We have talked about ways that having a sense of meaning can boost our resilience and help us handle stress and other challenges with a bit more ease. But reminding ourselves about our bigger why has another awesome benefit: it can elevate the most mundane everyday activities out of the ordinary and transform them into meaningful experiences that bring us joy. My ninety-three-year-old grandpa helped me learn this lesson.

When I took up painting a few years ago, my grandpa proudly told his artist friend about my new passion and said he'd bring me over for a visit. I promised to make a date to drive us to his friend's apartment, but I kept putting it off. I was juggling a lot and life was busy. Every time my grandpa asked me when we were going to see his friend, I made an excuse for why I couldn't do it then. I felt guilty, but my guilt wasn't strong enough to overcome my excuses.

One day when my grandpa was over for dinner, he saw my latest painting and said he liked it a lot. Suddenly, in that moment, I realized that for my grandpa, bringing me to meet his friend was more than just a social visit. He was proud of me and wanted to share his pride with a friend.

Two weeks later I picked him up and we drove to his friend's apartment. It took forever. There was tons of traffic and we couldn't find a place to park. But as his artist friend showed me some of his paintings—which were much more impressive than my work—and I showed him mine, I could see my grandpa glowing with pride. The moment meant so much to him. By extension, it meant a lot to me. What I had initially seen as something I *had* to do was transformed into something meaningful and joyful, an experience I was grateful to have. (True to my Russian Jewish roots, I also felt guilty about procrastinating and not doing this sooner. I can tell you with full confidence that guilt doesn't have the same benefits as having a bigger why.)

Gratitude and meaning are related. Both help us peel off the routine, shake up our emotional inertia, take the familiar wrapper off what we normally experience. While our gratitude practice enables us to appreciate small moments of joy and goodness in our day, connecting to our bigger why allows us to reframe some of what we already have to do into meaningful and purposeful activities.

There is an image I've seen going around Instagram and other social media sites that is a great visual for this. It's a photo of a list of household tasks:

I have to make dinner.

I have to clean up the kitchen.

I have to go grocery shopping.

I have to drive my kids to their activities.

And so on. But the message is in what's been crossed out. In each phrase, "have to" is crossed out and replaced with "get to."

I ~~have to~~ get to make dinner.

I ~~have to~~ get to clean up the kitchen.

I ~~have to~~ get to go grocery shopping.

I ~~have to~~ get to drive my kids to their activities.

By shifting our perception of a task we can often transform the most ordinary to-dos as well as stressful obligations into experiences that bring us a sense of purpose. Often they feel less burdensome as a result. I didn't just drive my grandpa to see his artist friend. I got to help my grandpa experience an awesome moment of pride. I didn't have to change my life or quit my job. I just had to connect what seemed at first like an obligation to my bigger why, my love for him and my desire to give him a moment of proud joy.

It's amazing how the most mundane activities take on a greater sense of meaning if we look at how they contribute to someone or something outside of ourselves. That also helps us experience more joy as we do them. In this way, cultivating our sense of purpose isn't just an important part of boosting our emotional immune system so we can get through challenges with greater resilience. It's also a powerful practice to help us find more moments of joy within our everyday moments.

*practice* **To-Do List Makeover**

We all have routine things we need to do, tasks that might be tedious or annoying. If you can connect each task with some bigger meaning, you may be able enjoy fulfilling them (even if just a little bit more).

For this exercise, take a look at your to-do list. Maybe it's on your phone, in your datebook, or even in your head. As you go through each task, consider how it might be helpful to someone else or contribute to a cause or project that you really care about.

You might ask yourself, *Does this help someone?* or *How is this in service of something that is meaningful to me?* When I do this practice, I find that my long to-do list becomes easier to tackle.

## The Pilgrimage Toward Meaning

If you already know what brings you meaning—or if you're discovering it right now—that is awesome. But it's also completely normal not to know what your purpose is. I often get emails from people who tell me they feel lost and don't know how to find meaning. I've felt that way in my own life as well.

If you don't yet know what gives you a sense of meaning, you can still explore. Or as Paulo Coelho did, you can pilgrimage toward it.

A few years ago I listened to an interview with Paulo Coelho, author of *The Alchemist,* which spent more than four hundred weeks on the *New York Times* bestseller list. *The Alchemist* tells the story of a young shepherd and his journey to Egypt to find treasure he believes is buried there. But more so, this book is an allegory, a story of the boy's journey within himself to find out what is truly meaningful and important in life. The book was inspired by Paulo Coelho's own journey toward becoming an author at the age of forty. It happened after he had gone on a pilgrimage across Northern Spain to Santiago de Compostela. It was at the end of this emotionally and physically difficult five-hundred-mile pilgrimage that he says he realized that he either had to pursue his dream of writing or forget it altogether. Many people are grateful he chose the former because his writing has deeply touched and inspired millions around the world (to date, the book has been translated into seventy-four languages). I'm one of those people.

In an interview with Krista Tippett on her *On Being* podcast, Paulo Coelho talked about how exploration and discovery are integral parts of life—including in defining what is meaningful. For example, he spoke about how he had tried all kinds of religions and different practices to understand which one felt right for him. He suggested that all of us can go on our own pilgrimage without having to travel to Egypt or Spain or anywhere far from where we live. He said:

> We have this possibility of doing a pilgrimage every single day. Because a pilgrimage implies meeting different people, talking to strangers, paying attention to the omens, and basically being open to life. And we

leave our home to go to work, to go to school, and we have every single day this possibility, this chance of discovering something new. So the pilgrimage is not for the privileged one who can go to Spain, and to France, and walk this five hundred miles, but to people who are open to life. A pilgrimage, at the end of the day, is basically a way to get rid of things that you are used to and try something new.

Paulo Coelho suggests that we treat our everyday lives as a pilgrimage that helps us discover what moves us, what is meaningful to us. He recommends being open to people, ideas, and circumstances you encounter as part of your days. If you have an inkling to try something, or if something piques your interest, pull on that thread. You might follow it long enough to realize you want to pursue it with more of your time and energy because it makes you feel that you're contributing to someone or something outside of yourself. Or you might follow it for a while and in the process discover another direction that calls to you. Your path to finding what gives you meaning is a combination of being curious, interested, and open to opportunities and your effort to explore them.

I've witnessed many people experience a sense of urgency when it comes to discovering their bigger why. They feel they should have it and are frustrated or sad that they don't. They send themselves into the Valley of Suffering, caught between how they are and how they've decided they should be. As long as we're stuck in the Valley of Suffering, it's difficult to move forward, have clarity, or be truly present to notice something that might lead us to our source of meaning.

Part of the search for our purpose is to practice acceptance: give yourself a break for not discovering it *yet*. The pressure to find your life meaning could be the very thing that may be preventing you from following your curiosity, your interests, or your gut instincts as you try different things. Who knows, if you relax that pressure, something unexpected might lead you to a key discovery. Being open means dropping your expectations of what's going to happen and listening deeply to yourself instead. By allowing yourself some room to explore without the need to *find that one thing right now* you may end up discovering your unique and best self.

I love the exploration that Lorraine Pascale went on to discover what brought her meaning. Lorraine is a well-known British chef who has appeared on television and has sold more than one million cookbooks. Lorraine reached out to say some incredibly kind things about my work through Happier. As we began to get to know each other, I became curious about how she became a chef. Was it something she always wanted to do?

Not at all, as it turns out. Before she was a chef, Lorraine was a successful model in Britain. While she enjoyed her work, she told me it lacked a sense of purpose. She had a difficult childhood, having been shuffled between different foster homes since she was just a baby. But she had warm memories of her father, a Spanish teacher who found a lot of meaning and happiness in his work. So Lorraine decided to give up her modeling career and find her own bigger why. She read *What Color Is Your Parachute?*—a bestseller by Richard N. Bolles about finding the right career—and made a list of all the things she liked doing. Then she tried to figure out if she could make a career out of any one of them. She loved cars, so she experimented with being a car mechanic, but it didn't feel right. Following her interest in the human brain, Lorraine became a master practitioner in neurolinguistic programming but eventually decided that wasn't the right path either. It was only after she took a course at a cooking school that she felt she found what she was searching for.

"I found my passion in baking. I knew it was right because I could not get enough of it. I would read all the books and cook all the time. And when I was doing it, I was at peace. I felt like I had come home," Lorraine said in her email to me.

But while Lorraine loves baking and has achieved tremendous success in her work, she told me that she feels that something is still missing, that "a little piece of my soul jigsaw is not quite right," as she put it. Her recipes help many people improve their cooking and eat really tasty food, but she feels a yearning to contribute in other ways as well. She is still undertaking her meaning pilgrimage and evolving her bigger why.

## Exploring Meaning

Whether you're still searching for your bigger why or feel you have discovered it, it's helpful to take a step back from time to time and allow yourself to explore. Set aside twenty or thirty minutes for this practice and give yourself permission to not worry about what ideas or thoughts come out. You might plant a seed for something that will bloom much later.

Psychologists identify four areas where we might experience meaning:

**Work/achievements.** Believing in what you're doing, finding it rewarding and challenging; feeling like you're contributing to something important and valuable through your work.

**Relationships/intimacy.** Feeling connected to others; helping and supporting them.

**Religion/spirituality.** Having a personal relationship with a higher power; feeling as if you're serving your life purpose in this lifetime; contributing to a spiritual community.

**Transcendence.** A sense that you're contributing to the society where you live, transcending your own self-interests and leaving a legacy.

As you read through these, take a few minutes to write in your journal. Write your response to or reflections on these questions:

- Do any of these four categories of meaning speak to you more than the others? (There's no right answer.)
- Are you actively creating meaning in any of these areas right now?
- Is there one that you're curious about and would like to explore further?

Identify a few simple ways you could begin to explore areas that you're curious about.

It feels great to connect to something that helps you share some of your best qualities, your truest self, and your most natural strengths with the world and help other people by doing that. I hope that the practices in this chapter have helped you get a little bit closer to feeling that way. But remember, just as Lorraine discovered on her pilgrimage toward meaning, it's not a one-time event—it's not like you find meaning once and it never changes or evolves, or if you can't pinpoint it right now you're doomed. Like the other core elements we have talked about, connecting to your bigger why is an ongoing practice, so give yourself the emotional room to learn and explore.

## Your Daily Anchors Check-In

Do a check-in with your daily anchors practice. What practices are helping you feel more content and joyful? Which ones support you when things aren't going great? Ask yourself these questions from time to time and adjust your daily anchors based on how you feel. Sometimes we need more of a joy boost, other times we need to find the strength to accept something difficult and work through it. It's absolutely okay to shift your daily anchors to suit your needs right now.

# 10

# Self-Care

Self-care is never a selfish act—it is simply good stewardship
of the only gift I have, the gift I was put on earth to offer others.
PARKER J. PALMER

I decided to include self-care as the last of the five core
practices for cultivating your happier skills because it
encompasses the first four practices within it. Self-care
means that you approach yourself with acceptance rather than
condemnation or harsh judgment, particularly when you make
a mistake or fail at something. It asks that you express gratitude to yourself for your strengths, your quirks, and your being.
Self-care means extending the same kindness and compassion
toward yourself as you would toward someone you care about,
and remembering that you have a purpose to serve and that
you can do it best when you nourish yourself and fuel your
mind, body, and soul. It isn't an extra or some bonus that you
earn after you work hard enough or achieve certain milestones.
It's an integral, necessary practice that helps you cultivate your
happier skills.

We can't feel good if we're physically and emotionally
drained. We can't get through the many times life throws us
curveballs if we're not taking care of ourselves. This seems like
an obvious idea and yet many of us put taking care of ourselves
toward the very bottom of our list of priorities.

So, pause for a minute and think about the kind of relationship you have with yourself. I don't recall a single time when I did this for most of my life. *You want me to think about how I treat myself? What a ridiculous idea.* That is what I used to think—*selfish*. At the rare times when I circled the topic, I just thought that I wasn't pushing myself hard enough, wasn't doing as much as I should, wasn't reaching as high or moving as fast to get there as I should have been. Exactly zero times did I think something crazy like *You should take care of yourself better. You should be kinder to yourself. You're good enough as you are.*

It never crossed my mind to treat myself with the kindness and care I tried to extend to my family and friends. I would tell them to take breaks, and I'd often try to steal them away for lunch or a walk. But I wouldn't take breaks myself. I loved surprising my husband and daughter with a beautiful dinner on a weeknight or turning a regular morning into one that felt a little less routine with their favorite breakfast. In the process, I exhausted myself by trying to make these surprises as perfect as possible. By no means was I a selfless human being who only ever thought about other people. I spent plenty of time feeling sorry for how exhausted and drained I felt (while at the same time berating myself for not working hard enough).

It took hitting rock bottom to give myself permission to spend time and energy to nurture myself. Why didn't I do it earlier? Because I didn't feel that I deserved it. The foundation of self-care is self-love, a belief that we're worth our own kindness and support. And I didn't love myself—I made that love conditional upon achieving enough, and I hadn't gotten to that *enough* yet.

My experience is hardly unique. It's amazing how many smart, kind, loving, successful people feel they don't deserve the love and care they extend to others. When I hesitantly began to share my struggle to be self-compassionate, I was blown away by the number of times I heard this kind of confession: "I don't feel that I deserve to take care of myself, to love myself, to be happy."

## From Self-Acceptance to Self-Love

Where do our feelings of unworthiness come from? Why is it easier to be kind to a friend or more understanding with a family member than with ourselves? In part, we struggle with feeling worthy of our own love and care because our negativity bias is masterful at spotting negative traits in ourselves. Think about it. What do you say to yourself more often: *I appreciate this aspect of myself or this behavior* or *This aspect of myself or my behavior should be different; I dislike it and I should have changed it already*. (I cringe thinking about the numbers of days I've started by looking in the bathroom mirror and immediately condemning some part of myself: *I hate the fat on my stomach! I should have gotten more done yesterday!*) It feels wrong, strange, not humble, not real to express gratitude to ourselves for ourselves. We're more comfortable taking the good stuff for granted. But the stories we create are extremely powerful. If we always hear about what's wrong and rarely about what's good (and beautiful, strong, bold, compassionate, creative), then no wonder so many of us don't feel worthy of our own love.

Of course, other people throughout our lives might contribute to our sense of unworthiness. But our own continual self criticism drives these feelings deeper. We just don't have to approach ourselves this way. We have a choice. The way toward realizing that we're worthy of our own love begins by giving ourselves permission to recognize our many good qualities and to take care of ourselves with the same care and compassion we reserve for other people we love.

At thirty-five, my friend Nondini had a successful career and was the CEO of a financial literacy company she helped found in Boston. She had a great circle of friends, loving parents who lived a few hours away, a brother she was close to. Yet almost from the moment we met I could sense a struggle in her. It turned out that Nondini's marriage had ended and she was going through a painful divorce.

Sometime after her divorce was finalized, Nondini began to date. At first, there was an urgency to it. She was hungry for a warm, loving relationship. But she also felt she *should* have one. Her younger brother was engaged to be married, and her parents, whom she loved very much, wanted her to be happily remarried. Nondini and her parents had always imagined that her life would be a certain way when she reached her midthirties: marriage, career, a house, maybe kids. Nondini met some nice men, but the dates didn't turn into meaningful relationships. She had a lot of doubt—about dating again, that someone else would love her, about her own ability to love herself. Sometimes this doubt would feel paralyzing to her, and I could so relate—the voice of doubt in her head echoed the vicious voice of doubt that dominated my thoughts for so many years.

One night on our way to dinner, she told me that she'd decided to remove her online dating profile. I was surprised, but she said it with a confidence I hadn't heard from her in a long while. She wanted to be solo for a while, to take time and space to heal and love who she was, just as Nondini herself, without a perfect relationship. Then she read me a letter she wrote to herself. Tears welled up in my eyes as I listened, but I was also happy for her. She was generous enough to give me permission to share her letter with you:

Dear Nondini,

I love you. I love you more than anyone else could ever love you. I will not abandon you. I will not leave you. I will not betray you.

You and I are building a relationship that cannot be severed.

As a gift to you, which is the part of me that is wounded and mourning and scared, I offer you this:

- I release you from the expectations of your ego. You do not have to be perfect for me to love you.
- I see all of you, know all of you, and I have known and been there for your every single mess-up and mistake. And I still love you and accept you as you are.
- I forgive you. I forgive you completely.
- I want to remove the pressure you put on yourself to look like everything is fine and that you have bounced back perfectly.
- That is why I am going to take down your dating profiles and the only expectation that I have of you going forward is that you will discover, learn, and fall in love with yourself.
- I know that this is the only pathway and the only way to find true happiness and peace. It is a gift that only we can give each other.
- I also give you the gift of not repeating the same mistakes and the same behaviors over and over again. I will not let other people use you as a revolving door and I will not let you see yourself in that way.
- I will stop judging you.
- If you feel pain I will sit with you and let you feel that pain. If you feel sadness I will sit with you and let you feel that sadness. When you are joyful and when you laugh—I will be by your side. I am committed to you

When you are ready, that is when we will head out into the world. United, whole, self-aware, and self-accepting.

That does not mean perfection.

It simply means that you will know who you are and what you want. And what will truly make you happy.

WITH LOVE, NONDINI

Nondini's letter was proof to herself that she deserved her own love. She didn't have to achieve it or make up for her past missteps or meet a new husband to be worthy of it—she was simply lovable as she was. Her letter was a reminder to the critical part of herself that she could ease up on her self-judgment, and that what she really craved and needed was already within reach: her self-acceptance.

You deserve your own love too. Not because you're perfect or have achieved enough of the right things, but because you're *you*, with all the complex and beautiful parts of you. Self-love asks that first you practice acceptance and learn how to see yourself clearly, with the flaws and mistakes and the awesome parts. Then you cultivate your ability to love yourself—not despite your flaws but inclusive of them. You learn to love your true being.

 *journal practice*

## Self-Gratitude

Spend a few minutes expressing gratitude to yourself for *yourself*. If you're having trouble getting started, imagine that someone who really cares about you is writing this. Here are a few questions to guide you. Let your answers be as specific as possible.

- What aspects of yourself do you really love and value?
- What are some ways you help others?
- How have you overcome a fear or done something challenging?

- How have you shown strength during a difficult time?
- What do you appreciate about how you navigate through life, even when you take a misstep or make a mistake?
- How have you grown emotionally, mentally, physically, or spiritually in the last year, two years, five years? What do you appreciate about this growth?

## Becoming Better Friends with Yourself

Think about people you love. Do they have flaws? The answer is probably yes. Have they ever made mistakes or done something that hurt you? Also, probably yes. Yet you still love them. You may get angry, upset, frustrated, sad, disappointed at them at times, but you don't withdraw your love.

"You're a being, not a doing," Janet said to me one day when I was struggling with her suggestion that I practice loving and accepting myself just as I am. *But I'm not always kind or forgiving,* I argued, *and I've hurt people I love and I've not achieved enough and . . .*

"Those are things you might have done," she said calmly. "And we all have ways we've screwed up and ways we can improve. I'm not asking you to love everything you do but to love who you are, your being."

While I understood what Janet meant, I had trouble putting her words into practice—I couldn't separate my being from all the things I've done, including my many mistakes. But one day, shortly after my meeting with Janet, I had a flash of clarity. Mia and I were running outside to my car, which was parked in front of our house on a freezing Boston winter day. When I tried to open the door, I realized I'd forgotten my keys in the house. Under my breath, I mumbled angrily at myself, "You're so stupid! How dumb is it to forget your keys when you know it's so cold!"

Mia was looking straight at me, and in that moment I had a realization that set me on a path to try to practice self-compassion. I recognized that I would never react that way to her if she had made a small mistake like this. I love her unconditionally and wouldn't treat her with that same knee-jerk harshness. (I was also struck by the awareness that how I treat myself is setting up a model for how Mia might learn to treat herself as she grows up, and I would never want her to be this harsh.)

Simply put, self-compassion means that we treat ourselves as we would treat a good friend or someone we care about. If a friend makes a mistake or fails at something, do you berate them? Scream at them? Tell them they're an awful failure and will be forever? Of course not—you wouldn't want to make them feel worse. You probably comfort your friend, extend kindness, and remind them that this isn't the end of the world and they can get through it. Do you treat yourself this way?

At the heart of self-compassion is the way we talk to ourselves. Remember the voice in your head from the chapter about acceptance? When we practice becoming aware of our thoughts, we often discover that the voice in our head can be incredibly harsh. It can be so cruel that it keeps us from experiencing the good in many of our daily moments. It's often total joy-kill and incredibly deflating. Gretchen, whose stressful job involves managing multiple projects and teams, was taking my course on self-compassion when she emailed me this insight:

> When I run into an obstacle during work, I start to immediately beat myself up about it because I feel like I didn't get everything done as perfectly as I should have. Which then makes me feel like I'm not good enough and that just ruins my spirit. It's like this never-ending cycle. I can't even celebrate small victories because I keep thinking that I could have done something better.

Gretchen also mentioned in our email exchange that while she tries to be encouraging and kind toward people she works with, even when they make mistakes, she feels that doing the same for herself is like letting herself off the hook. I can absolutely relate. One of the biggest issues I had with self-compassion was that it felt like the enemy of achievement and self-improvement. Personally, I preferred investing my energy in beating myself up rather than letting myself off lightly. This is the objection I hear from so many people: "If I'm super nice and gentle with myself, then I'll never improve at anything!"

But self-compassion isn't about ignoring our mistakes or failures or trying to see them through fake rosy sunglasses. Self-compassion doesn't mean we give ourselves a pass and just don't care about what we do or how we might affect other people. Rather, it's rooted in the same place where our compassion and kindness toward others come from: a desire to reduce suffering and improve well-being. Mark Leary, a professor of psychology and neuroscience at Duke University, offers a useful insight in his article about self-compassion for *Aeon* magazine titled "Don't Beat Yourself Up." "Self-compassionate people want to reduce their current problems," he writes, "but they also want to respond in ways that promote their well-being down the road, and being lazy and unmotivated is not likely to help."

In fact, research shows that self-compassion *increases* motivation. In one study that Leary describes, researchers Juliana Breines and Serena Chen, both from the University of California, Berkeley, gave participants who failed an initial test another chance to improve their scores. Those who thought about their initial failure in a self-compassionate way studied 25 percent longer and scored higher on the second test than participants who focused on increasing their self-esteem. Reacting to failure with self-compassion *reduces* our fear of failure because we don't beat ourselves up as harshly, so we're more willing to try again and to try even harder.

Think for a minute about how you talk to yourself if you make a mistake or fail at achieving a goal. Do you berate yourself and beat yourself up? If you do, do you feel motivated or inspired to try a different approach or work harder? I think if we're honest with ourselves, most of us would say no. When we approach ourselves with compassion, on the other hand, we can see more clearly where we might have gone wrong, what we should do differently, and, perhaps most importantly, fuel ourselves with positive energy to try again.

*practice* **Reframing Harsh Self-Talk**

Here is a simple three-step practice to help you shift from negative to more compassionate self-talk:

**Step 1   Listen.** Be mindful of the words and tone you use when you talk to yourself. Practice witnessing your self-talk as it happens. What is the tone like? What words or phrases do you use when you talk to yourself?

**Step 2   Pause.** When you catch yourself engaged in negative self-talk, take a breath and pause for a second. In this pause, connect to your inner witness. Feel the depth of your capacity to be aware of your thoughts and emotions without the need to immediately react.

**Step 3   Reframe.** Imagine you're talking to someone you really love and care about. Visualize this person and hold them in your heart's attention. Now begin to reframe what you said to yourself and how you said it, imagining that you're talking to this person.

## Making Self-Care Routine

Learning how to practice self-compassion, including talking to ourselves in a kinder way, is an integral part of self-care. But there are other elements. What helps you to feel nourished? Eating healthy, getting sleep, exercising, spending time outside, meditating, catching up with friends, sitting in a café for an hour and people-watching, reading, journaling, or something else? Your self-care practice is a way to refuel so that you have the emotional and physical energy to thrive, including getting through times when life isn't going great. Self-care should be something you *want* to do rather than feel obligated to accomplish. It's your time to be a really good friend to yourself and take yourself on a tiny little vacation within the routine of your everyday responsibilities.

To prevent your long list of to-dos from sabotaging your self-care, you have to treat it with some discipline. Because even if you overcome the guilt obstacle many of us run into—feeling as if you don't deserve to be nice to yourself or feeling guilty about taking time just for you—self-care can get lost behind all the other responsibilities you have on your plate. It's so easy to put ourselves last. My friend Sharon recently launched a new company while also working through some family priorities that needed her attention. She felt overwhelmed, and when I asked what she was doing just for herself, she admitted she struggled with that. "I feel that taking care of me comes in place of taking care of others," she said. We can all relate—there are only so many hours in the day. But what I told her in response is the same thing I tell myself whenever I feel that there isn't time to take care of myself or the voice of guilt in my head gets too loud: you can't give what you don't have.

We might think that we can run our wells of emotional and physical energy dry and still take care of people we care about, do great work, excel at our studies, or manage our priorities.

But it's just not possible, not for longer than a short while. We have to take care of ourselves to be able to take the best care of the people and things that matter to us. One of the best ways to avoid making self-care last on our list is to make it a regular part of our routines, a steadfast component of our daily anchors.

I asked Chetan, my friend whose burnout I shared with you in part 1, to tell me how he finally made caring for himself a priority. His answer surprised me. Maybe because he's a natural entrepreneur, he chose to approach it just the way he approaches all his work. "I think the biggest shift was treating self-care like a job," he said. "That sounds a little drab, but it was absolutely critical for it to work for me."

It feels strange to talk about taking care of ourselves as yet another task. But if you don't become disciplined about it—if you don't elevate it to the same level of importance as your work or taking care of other people—the voice in your head will find opportunities to sabotage even your best intentions.

When I asked people who participated in my class on self-compassion why they weren't doing better at self-care, here is what I heard:

> I know yoga makes me feel really good and helps me to recharge, but I just get caught up in getting other stuff done and don't make it to class.

> I feel so much better when I get a run or a brisk walk in, but I end up catching up on work after the kids are in bed and don't get out often.

> I know how important it is to get good sleep and how much better I function when I do, but there's just so much to do, to write, to read, that I often get to bed too late.

So, I think Chetan is on to something when he talks about treating self-care like a job, with the same degree of consistency, planning, and discipline. Here is how he approached getting better sleep:

> I never used to be very rigorous about my sleep. I kind of enjoyed the mental image of myself as a relaxed person, and I told myself I do my best work at night. But in fact, nighttime was the only time that I was carving out for uninterrupted work. When I set a target bedtime for myself of 11:00 p.m., and committed to a goal of getting seven and a half hours of sleep, I started getting much more and much better quality sleep. I wasn't perfect, and it took about three months to get into the rhythm, but getting consistent sleep has made a huge difference—I feel better and get more done.

Chetan had to reckon more honestly with himself. What he wanted was to function well on too little sleep, but the reality was that he needed more rest. His work depended on it, and he saw results from getting better quality sleep.

What Chetan noticed when he finally got serious about getting more rest was that he couldn't change his habits overnight. That applies to almost all of us. When you want to make a change, even one that makes you feel good, it might take practice until it becomes more natural. Research shows that when it comes to creating a new habit, motivation is a lot less important than consistency. When I want to change a habit, I lean on the Fogg Method, developed by BJ Fogg, a behavioral scientist and professor at Stanford University. It's simple. Here is how it works:

**Step 1**  Set a specific goal with a short time frame. Think less *I'm going to take better care of myself* and more *I'm going to go to yoga class on Saturday afternoons for one month.*

**Step 2**  Make it very simple to start. You're much more likely to stick to a self-care habit if it's something reasonable and doable. Instead of committing to going to yoga five days a week, how about starting with just one class on the weekend.

**Step 3**  Come up with a trigger to remind yourself to do it. In the yoga class example, this can mean putting on your yoga clothes first thing in the morning or keeping your yoga mat by the door.

I'm only using yoga as an example here, not a specific prescription (although I do love it). You may not be interested in yoga but enjoy walking, ceramics, playing on a local dodgeball team, or meeting friends more regularly. Once you identify a few activities that help nourish and fuel you, you can apply these steps from the Fogg Method to start to integrate them into your routine.

Your self-care practice doesn't have to be complicated or difficult. It can be as simple as taking ten minutes to sit quietly and drink your morning coffee or tea in peace before you start your day. Here is a great example from Tanya, a senior project manager at a national nonprofit, who responded when I shared with the Happier community my struggle to become more self-compassionate:

> I used to wear stress as a status symbol and prided myself for being able to work absurd hours for days on end. After many episodes of this mentality driving me to physical illness, I finally got a wake-up call. At the Democratic National Convention in

July 2016, I worked a twenty-hour day. It was an exciting and intense atmosphere and I had a high-stakes role to play. By the end of the day, however, my body, mind, and spirit were so drained that I wound up in the emergency room with an allergic reaction. None of the doctors could identify a food or physical allergen. It seemed likely that stress was the culprit. That was a loud and clear message that I had to stop sacrificing my health for work, no matter how important my job seemed.

My proudest takeaway from that moment is that I separated my identity from work and located my worth within myself. With this newfound freedom to feel worthy just for being me, I am able to give myself the flexibility to add creative time and rest into my workdays. I've arranged with my superiors to be able to work from home on certain days. I turn off screens at 10:00 p.m. (well, on most nights). I practice morning and evening rituals that fuel and soothe me—and I don't beat myself up when I miss them.

And, as counterintuitive as it may sound, taking it easier has actually increased my productivity!

## Creating Your Self-Care Ritual

What nourishes you? Spend a few minutes making a list of activities that make you feel refreshed, energized, or more calm and centered. They can be things you're already doing regularly or haven't done in a while.

Now, could you pick one that you'd like to stick to more regularly? Check out the three steps above and write out how you'll start to apply them to the activity that you chose. How will you make this into a regular self-care ritual?

## Giving Yourself Permission to Rest

Did you catch that last line in Tanya's email in the last section? The part where she talked about taking it easier and becoming more productive? If I hadn't had a similar experience, I would have dismissed it as totally impossible. But deep down we all know, even the workaholics among us, that Tanya is right. How much awesomeness can you bring to the world when you're drained, exhausted, and overwhelmed?

On a recent episode of *Hidden Brain*, one of my favorite podcasts, host Shankar Vedantam shared a story about Katie, a bright young doctor. Always determined and hardworking, Katie devoted all her time and energy to her job. As a resident, she often worked sixteen hours a day, then went home, exercised to keep her body healthy, did some reading, and got a few hours of sleep. She cut out everything else from her life, including eating enough or spending time with friends.

As you can probably guess, Katie couldn't keep this up. Eventually, she noticed that she had many near misses at work. For example, she almost forgot to prescribe insulin for a diabetic patient. Not eating more than some fruits and vegetables on most days brought her back to the battle she'd had with eating disorders when she was younger. Soon, Katie couldn't function well at all and checked into a rehab facility for people with eating disorders.

One of the things she was required to do in this facility was—nothing. No sneaking in exercise, no work, not even jumping jacks. At first Katie described how angry she became. Negative thoughts filled her mind. But slowly she relaxed into doing nothing because she had no choice. She realized that she felt more peaceful. She started painting and drawing and fell in love with making art. She learned not to push herself so hard and to be okay with that.

After she got better, Katie returned home and converted one of the small rooms in her house to an art room. She started to spend a few hours there every week, just creating, with no other goal in mind. A few nights a week she schedules a date night with herself, to watch a movie, go for a walk, or do something else she enjoys, by herself.

When Katie returned to her job, she discovered something surprising: she had a much greater capacity to remember things and could get a lot more done. It was like her mind had expanded. Working less and taking time to rest, to do things that helped rejuvenate her body and spirit, had done more to help Katie become better at her job than pushing herself had.

I know only too well where Katie was coming from. I, too, had to learn how to rest and to use all my acceptance and self-compassion skills to calm the voice in my head that objected to my "useless" behavior: *Only weak people take breaks! If you start taking them, it means you're weak and lazy! You'll get nothing done, ever!* To my surprise, when I started to rest more, I found that, like Chetan, I began to get more done and do it better. The year following my commitment to self-care turned out to be the most creative year of my life—and I'm generally a creative person. This has benefited my work, my writing, my family, my friends, and my soul. (There, I said it: *soul!*)

Perhaps most importantly, for the first time I felt as if my work was fueling me rather than draining me. I didn't do any less of it. In some ways, I did more. But I did it differently: from a place of love—for my work, for my bigger why, for the people it benefited, and for me—rather than from a place of fear. For so long I had been afraid that if I didn't do enough, well enough, and fast enough, then I wouldn't be enough. My determination and persistence were still there. What changed is the way I use them and how I treat myself.

There is increasing scientific evidence that supports the benefits of rest that Katie and I have experienced, particularly the ways in which doing less can help us become more creative and productive. When we focus on solving a problem and then take a break from it, our subconscious brain keeps thinking about it. That is why we often literally come up with great ideas in the shower: it's a place where we feel relaxed and allow our conscious brain to take a break. Scientists call this the incubation period. Our subconscious mind has been working on solving the problem in the background, and when we allow the part of our brain we use for focusing and problem solving (our frontal cortex) to disconnect, the subconscious mind has the opportunity to share its solutions and ideas.

It turns out that the brain is still working when we take mental breaks—and often working in ways that we simply can't access unless we hit pause on the endless cycle of doing, email checking, reading, going to meetings, and other activities we normally consider "productive." One of the critical tasks the brain accomplishes when we give it a break from having to take in new information is to reflect on and organize what it has recently learned. This is crucial. When you get a good night's sleep, for example, do you feel like you can do things better and faster, that your brain is sharper and you can get more things done? Your brain *is* sharper because it has had time to do all that reflecting and organizing. Naps have similar benefits. One study that looked at four years of data on highway car accidents involving Italian policemen found that when they took a short nap before starting their night shift, they reduced their risk of getting into collisions by 48 percent.

If you hesitate to take time to rest because it feels as if you're doing nothing, remind yourself that your brain is doing a whole lot. Rather than thinking about rest as empty space devoid of productivity, consider it a necessary ingredient in optimizing your capacity as a human being to work, care for people you love, and share your gifts with the world.

Dana, a marketing professional and member of the Happier community, writes about how doing something other than work helps her to be more creative:

> I quit my corporate marketing job a year ago so that I could go into private practice, work three days a week, and spend the other days with my babies. It has been the biggest inner struggle to truly be present with my kiddos on those days and not be glued to my phone. I hate the guilt associated with taking that time to be with them and had completely forgotten that taking time away from work fuels my most important asset—my creativity!

She's not imagining it: studies show that we're more creative when we're relaxed and producing more dopamine in our brain, giving us another reason to take rest seriously. In one study, researchers from the National Institutes of Health scanned the brains of freestyle rappers using functional MRI to see what parts of their brains were activated as they invented their rhythms and lyrics on the spot. As they were improvising, the rappers had less activity in their frontal lobes, suggesting that creativity requires that our executive functions take a backseat. When the brain becomes less focused on solving problems, there is more opportunity for free association and unexpected connections. Another word for that is *creativity*, the next important element of self-care that I want to share with you.

## Scheduling Rest

Schedule some time to spend with yourself doing something relaxing. It can be anything from taking a long walk to spending an hour at your favorite coffee shop with a book, or just hanging out at home with some magazines and favorite snacks. Even a half hour or an hour of time off from work and responsibilities can make a huge difference. Block the time off on your calendar so you can look forward to it and reduce your inclination to skip it.

Take a few moments to reflect on how you feel after you take a break and consider writing about this in your journal:

- Do you feel more motivated to take up your responsibilities?
- Are you more productive?
- Do you feel refreshed and more able to deal with stress?

Being more aware of the positive ways that rest contributes to your life will help you commit to this practice on a regular basis. And it's a great way to calm the voice in your head if it tries to make you feel guilty about resting.

## Fueling Up with Creativity

I've always loved art—seeing it, learning about it, experiencing it, and creating it. I've dabbled with abstract painting over the years, completing maybe ten paintings. But I've always wanted to paint. Really paint, with oil, or watercolor, or acrylic, or anything else. It's something that has been calling to me for decades. Mostly I ignored it.

I'd begun my practice of self-compassion the year before my fortieth birthday, but things were still pretty rough. As a part of my self-care efforts, I made a list of things I wanted to do for myself. To paint in Tuscany was at the top of the list. I'd never been to Tuscany, but I had this dreamy idea of painting outside, in a huge sun hat and white dress, with the green of Tuscan hills surrounding me. I must have conjured it up after watching the movie *Under the Tuscan Sun*—wasn't it fabulous?—but nevertheless, there it was on my list. After much encouragement from a dear friend, I decided to make the journey to mark my big upcoming birthday.

Yes, I went to Tuscany to paint. For two weeks. Of course, my negative self-talk had a good time with this—*Going on this trip all by yourself! My, my. It's SO expensive! You're being very self-indulgent! Why do you deserve to do this?* But the experience was so life changing that I was able to quiet the voice down after a while.

Finally giving myself something I dearly wanted opened the floodgates. My passion for painting burst out of me with a force I hadn't experienced in a long time. I noticed that when I painted, the chatter in my head slowed down. Now when I paint, it feels like I'm taking a vacation from my head. I feel more awake to the world around me, more in the flow of life.

Psychologist Mihaly Csikszentmihalyi has written extensively about the state of "flow" that we reach when we take part in an activity that is intrinsically rewarding for us, such as doing something creative. When we experience it, we often feel as if time has stopped and we have gotten completely immersed in what we're doing. It's the ultimate experience of being mindful and awake to the present moment, and one that helps us take a break from listening so closely to the voice in our head. Many people describe being immersed in doing something creative as similar to meditating. That has absolutely been my experience.

A growing body of research shows a link between creativity and improved emotional health. In one study, Tamlin Conner, a researcher at the University of Otago in New Zealand, and her colleagues analyzed online diaries that 650 young adults kept for two weeks. The study participants reported how much time they spent doing something creative every day and how much negative or positive emotion they experienced. The researchers found that the day *after* they engaged in creative activities the participants experienced more positive emotions—doing something creative literally helped them feel happier. (The study didn't find that experiencing more positive emotions one day led to more creative activities the following day, leading researchers to suggest that creativity *caused* positive feelings and wasn't just associated with them.)

*practice*

## Simple Ways to Explore Your Creativity

Come up with one simple way that you can explore your creativity in the coming weeks. Here are a few ideas to inspire you:

**Create a one-word journal.** The talented photographer Karen Walrond inspired me with this simple idea: Every day, for however long you want, write down in your journal one word that captures your day and decorate it somehow. No rules or requirements—just think of one word that captures the spirit of your day and add some doodles, colors, or stickers to help make it feel more alive.

**Make disappearing art.** One of the things that intimidates many people from being creative is the fear that the final product won't be good. What if you created art with the intention of not making the final outcome permanent? Andy Goldsworthy is an artist famous for creating landscape art pieces—huge ephemeral installations made completely from natural elements such as stones or sheep's wool. They're not meant to be permanent but to disappear with time. Reading about his art inspired me to try it. Since then I've made snow art with simple water-based paints and "sculptures" from tree branches, rocks, and leaves meant to be blown away by the wind. It's liberating to create something you know will be gone soon after you make it. (My daughter loves making these ephemeral art installations with me—it's a really fun project to try with kids.)

**Plant surprise inspiration.** My friend Ashley Longshore, who is an audaciously original artist, once mentioned this idea to me. I loved it immediately. Cut out some images, photographs, and quotes that inspire you. Take your planner, journal, or organizer and, without thinking or planning too much, decorate the pages for upcoming days, weeks, and months with the images you cut out. Add some motivating reminders, self-compassion mantras, or other things that make your soul sing. As you go through your days, you'll be surprised by all this inspiration you created for yourself.

**Stage a mystery basket cook-off.** Avi, Mia, and I love to watch *Chopped*, the Food Network show on which contestants get a basket of random ingredients to make their winning meals. You, too, can try this at home! Have a family member or friend pick five to ten random ingredients and try to make a dish out of them. Then switch places. It's silly, creative, spontaneous, and really fun. I plan our meals every week to make cooking and shopping manageable, and it's easy to get into a rut. This is an entertaining way to shake up your food and cooking routine, even if the dishes you create aren't culinary masterpieces.

**Embark on bookstore adventures.** One of my favorite things to do is to browse the aisles in a bookstore. Just reading the titles, seeing the book covers, and flipping through some pages fills me with this sense of possibility and gives me a bunch of ideas to think about. Take some time to browse around your local bookstore or library. Don't try to do anything, just browse. If something inspires you—to read, to write, to create—great. If not, give it a little time. Often the creative seeds you plant grow more slowly than you anticipate.

For most of my life I ignored my calling to paint. I considered it an "extra," an unnecessary and undeserved luxury, just like self-care. My extremely narrow perspective went something like this: *Since I'm not going to make a profession out of this or make money to help support my family, I shouldn't invest much time and energy into it.* I didn't feel I could afford "the distraction."

I know I'm not alone in feeling this way. Here is an email Susan, a member of the Happier community, sent me on this topic:

> I've had this vague feeling of disenchantment for six months now—just going through the motions, not really being here. I took time off from writing and painting classes recently, due to dealing with a troubled child in our family. I work in medicine so those are not my vocations; they were my creative hobbies. I just felt I should be more available to my husband and family during this awful time and I assumed the "ugh" I was feeling was the issues our son is dealing with.
>
> But I was wrong. By ignoring my flow, I've been bringing a hollowed-out soul to the table.
>
> I can't fix this child who is troubled, I can't even make my hair behave most days! But I can feed my soul and bring wholeness back into my life. So today, before work, I am starting with blue—I love the colors of blue and already I can feel the flow.

You can only starve your soul for so long. I wish I had given myself the permission to do more art sooner in my life, that I hadn't waited until I went through my darkest hour or had a big milestone birthday coming up. Whatever it is that helps you feel whole, in the flow, immersed in doing something you love, it's not an extra. It's part of the essential fuel to help you live your best life, to help you experience more joy and share it with others.

## Your Daily Anchors Check-In

We have now explored the five core practices that help you cultivate your happier skills, so this is a great time to pause and reflect on your daily anchors. How is it going for you? Do you find that you can do some or all your practices on most days? If yes, and you feel they're helping you cultivate a genuine sense of well-being, wonderful! If no, it's worth thinking about why. Perhaps you made your list too long. Or perhaps some of the practices aren't working so well for you. Remember that while you want to give each practice some time to marinate before you remove it from your list, you should also adjust your daily anchors so they work for *you.*

# Five-Minute Happier Workout

I've created this simple workout to help you practice all five core practices we have explored together in part 2 of this book. You may already be engaging in many of these practices as part of your daily anchors, which is awesome. But I want to share this workout with you as another suggestion for how you could practice your happier skills, especially if you only have a few minutes.

I recommend doing your Five-Minute Happier Workout in the morning, if possible, since research shows that the way we start our day significantly impacts how the day goes, including how we feel. But if that is not possible, no worries: simply try to find a time that works for you. It's better to do this short workout at any time than to not do it at all.

**Step 1  Acceptance.** Spend one or two minutes being still and silent. Just hit pause on your day and be. Take a few deep breaths, become aware of your body in space. Close your eyes if you can. Be who you are right now, witnessing your thoughts and feelings without judgment, without feeling bad or needing to fix anything.

**Step 2  Gratitude.** Think about two or three things you're grateful for right now. Be specific and capture what you're grateful for in some way—write it down, take a photo, say it, or text it to someone else.

**Step 3  Intentional kindness.** Do something kind. It can be as simple as texting a friend to check in. You can also combine gratitude with intentional kindness by sending an email or text to someone you appreciate and telling them why you feel that way. If you can't do something kind now, make a plan and set an intention to do it later in the day. Try to be specific about what you will do.

**Step 4  The bigger why.** Think about a few things you have to get done today and how they might serve your purpose. For example, is something on your to-do list helping another person? Sharing one of your strengths with others? Helping you hone your craft or skill?

**Step 5  Self-care.** Spend a few seconds talking to yourself in a supportive, kind way. If you're facing a challenge, remind yourself that you're more likely to get through it if you treat yourself with compassion rather than harshness. You can also take this time to think of one thing you'll do today to nourish yourself.

When you're done, say *thank you* to yourself for sticking to your commitment and for taking some time to cultivate your happier skills. You're awesome for making the choice to do this—for *you*!

(I've done this workout with many small and large teams at all kinds of companies and organizations and the feedback has always been incredibly positive, both in terms of how effective it is and how little time it takes. So if you're part of a team—or group, class, or community or religious organization—I encourage you to try this together!)

# 11

# Becoming a Force of Good
# in the World

*Thousands of candles can be lighted from a single candle,*
*and the life of the candle will not be shortened.*
*Happiness never decreases by being shared.*

BUDDHA

I hope that what you have read and practiced over the course of the previous chapters has inspired you to commit to cultivating your happier skills. I want to offer you one more important reason to stay on your path and keep up with your daily anchors: When you cultivate your well-being, your happiness, contentment, and joy can spread to other people. It spreads not because you make *them* change, but because *you*—your outlook and behavior—have changed. Think about how incredible that is! You not only have an opportunity to experience a genuine, lasting kind of happiness yourself, but you also just might help people in your life do the same. You don't have to do anything other than *practice* what we have talked about.

Nicholas A. Christakis, a professor at Yale University, and James Fowler, who teaches at the University of California, San Diego, have conducted several landmark studies showing that behavior and moods, including happiness, can be contagious within our social networks. For example, they found that when you become happier, a friend living close by has a 25 percent higher chance of becoming happier. (In their study, a spouse experienced an 8 percent increase in their chances of being happier while a next-door neighbor increased 34 percent.) Researchers have also found this to be true at work: employees who report having a strong sense of well-being are 20 percent more likely to have other colleagues on their team who are happier.

As we discussed earlier, a mountain of research shows that improving your emotional health has concrete and wide-reaching benefits, from reducing your risk of heart attacks and strokes and lowering your stress and anxiety to increasing your productivity and creativity. Because happiness is contagious, when you experience these benefits, your social network does too. When I began to write this book, I asked Avi, Mia, and some friends to tell me if they feel that the inner work that I've done over the past few years has impacted them in some way. Wow, was it heartwarming to hear their responses! I was overwhelmed when they told me not only about the positive changes they've seen in me but also how they've become more accepting of themselves (including when things aren't going well), more attentive to small moments of daily joy, better about taking care of themselves, more inspired to follow their passions and interests. Whenever my commitment to any of the practices I've shared with you wavers, I remind myself of how my own happier skills benefit the people I care most about.

## We're All Connected

Nicholas Christakis's work suggests something else surprising: happiness can spread *beyond* our nearby friends and neighbors or other people we come in contact with. When you become happier, the social network effect of happiness can spread up to three degrees, even reaching friends of friends.

In other words, we're all connected. And happiness is one of the best inputs into the web of relationships that connects all of us because it brings with it so many emotional and physical benefits. The healthier, stronger, kinder, and happier your network becomes, the healthier, stronger, kinder, and happier you become.

Consider how kindness spreads. Studies show that when we witness a compassionate or kind act, we feel more optimistic and are more likely to be kind to others. Researchers call this effect "moral elevation." As Adam Grant writes in *Give and Take: Why Helping Others Drives Our Success*, your acts of giving can change the nature of your social network to be more giving. He mentions how one study found that when one person made a choice to give to others consistently, other people in the group were more likely to contribute in the future, even when they weren't interacting with the original giver. By being kind, you increase the kindness level in your network, making it more likely that help will be there at a time when you need it.

Similarly, when we find the courage not just to accept our emotions but to share them without the "everything is okay" filter, we give people in our lives permission to do the same. It's as if we're literally saying, "I'm going to be honest about something that is not okay in my life so that it is safe for you to share what is not okay in yours." One of the powerful ways in which we can share the gift of acceptance with others is simply by practicing it ourselves and being honest about it.

Google recently released the findings of a five-year study it conducted to understand what makes some teams at Google perform so much better than others. After looking at the obvious potential factors—performance rankings for people on the team, pay scales, length of time at Google, and more—the researchers didn't find a common variable. But when they started to look into how the people on the team interacted rather than who the people were, they found the answer: psychological safety.

Psychological safety means that members of a team have a shared belief that they can be real and honest with each other, that they can express their ideas and emotions without the fear of being humiliated. As Harvard Business School professor Amy C. Edmondson defines it, "Psychological safety describes a team climate characterized by interpersonal trust and mutual respect in which people are comfortable being themselves."

Psychological safety creates that sacred space in which any team member can reveal that they're not okay and receive support from other team members. In the *New York Times* article about this study, one of the midlevel managers at Google, Matt Sakaguchi, described how he decided to practice psychological safety with his team. At a brainstorming session, he shared that he had been battling cancer, something he had kept from his colleagues until that point. At first the team was silent. But then people started sharing difficult things in their own lives, from an ongoing health issue to a difficult breakup. Sakaguchi described that when it came time to talk about ways to improve how their team worked together, his colleagues had a more honest, authentic, and useful conversation than any other time before. By taking the first step to share that he was not okay, Sakaguchi gave his colleagues an opportunity not only to support him, but also to become more honest themselves, something that ultimately served the whole team. Once he shared, Sakaguchi's personal practice of acceptance, including being okay with not being okay, influenced the culture of the entire team.

Imagine if we could all do this for the teams in our lives, including our families, friends, colleagues, classmates, or organizations in which we're involved. What might be possible?

For the majority of my daughter's life, I thought it was my job to protect her from feeling stress and witnessing my own stress or sadness. One day, a few years back, I came home from a really terrible, no-good, very bad day at work. Someone on my team had quit, a potential partnership fell through, a friend disappointed me, I had a terrible call with an investor, and the traffic on the way home was horrendous. Usually, when my daughter asked me how my day was, I would always say some version of "Okay!" But this time everything I felt was just too overwhelming and I told her the truth. "It was kind of awful, actually," I said.

As soon as the words left my mouth I felt a sense of panic. *I broke the golden rule of always seeming okay to my child!* But the world didn't end. My daughter didn't collapse. She hugged me and asked me if I wanted some tea. We shared tea and snacks at the kitchen table, played some cheesy music we both like, and went on with our night.

A few weeks after, I asked my daughter how her day was at school.

"It was alright, not great," she said.

My mom antenna went right up. "Why, what happened?"

"Nothing, really. I just didn't have a great day. I don't know."

This was the first time my daughter *ever* told me she didn't have a good day at school. She was eleven at the time. I suspect that the only reason that she finally did it was because I'd told her about my not-good day a few weeks earlier. By being more honest about my "not okay" I'd given her permission to embrace being "not okay." I had to hold my tongue to not try to cheer her up right away. It went against my instinct as her mom to not help her move through not feeling good as fast as possible. I knew how important it was to give her permission to feel how she felt, without the pressure to feel better.

Brené Brown, a research professor at the University of Houston Graduate College of Social Work who has studied vulnerability for two decades, and whose TED Talk, "The

Power of Vulnerability," has been viewed almost thirty million times (including ten times by me), says, "The difficult thing is that vulnerability is the first thing I look for in you and the last thing I'm willing to show you. In you, it's courage and daring. In me, it's weakness."

I was scared to share how not okay I was with anyone, including friends and family. I was afraid of seeming weak, and I was also hesitant to burden those I loved with my darkness. Yet seeing how my willingness to be more vulnerable created the space for my daughter to do the same, I was motivated to keep finding the courage to share what was real. I didn't always have to put on a brave face.

## The Power to Heal the World

"People who feel a sense of inner peace don't start wars," said Thom Knoles, a meditation teacher whose workshop I once attended in New York City. "Meditation helps you feel more peaceful and content. When you feel that way, you're much more likely to do good things for this world than bad things."

People who are happier don't start wars, either. They help people around them feel more joy and kindness because, as research shows, happiness and kindness spread. Happier people create safe spaces for others to be okay with not being okay because they cultivate psychological safety within their networks. They invent solutions to problems because feeling happier creates a mindset of possibility. People who are happier—truly, genuinely happier from within—become a force of good in their world.

You can become a force of good in our world.

This is my answer to even the biggest skeptics who come to my talks or read my emails and challenge the importance of investing their energy in becoming happier. This is my answer to anyone who, as I did for so long, feels that any kind of happiness that you don't earn through suffering is worthless and self-indulgent. This is my answer to anyone who doesn't feel they deserve to feel happier.

Cultivating your ability to experience more acceptance, joy, kindness, and meaning in everyday moments and learning to be okay when not everything is okay is the least selfish thing you can do. It's an amazing and unique gift that you automatically share with people you love, and even people you don't know—anyone who is part of this vast, complex human network that is the very fabric that supports us.

But you have to start within yourself.

To become a force of good in the world, to help people you care about live happier, more meaningful and fulfilling lives, you first have to cultivate these skills within yourself. As good as some of us may be at pretending—to be happy when we're not, to be okay when we're not—we're ultimately only pretending to ourselves. The real, deep, genuine truth of how we feel is what people around us sense and what we spread to them.

You may have to take baby steps at first, trying out your new skills on other people until they become second nature. Once, during a retreat in Utah, I took a yoga class with Elena Brower, a well-known yoga teacher. Something about her manner made me feel at ease, as if I could try out my practice of being okay with not being okay on her. We went for breakfast with some other folks from the class afterward. As part of the conversation, I admitted a few things that I was struggling with.

"I *so* get it!" Elena exclaimed. "We all struggle and we all try to hide it. I hid my smoking from everyone for years. Coming out about it was the scariest and most liberating thing I'd ever done. It felt like a release to admit to being so imperfect." Others around the table were nodding.

I didn't know Elena, but when I looked her up after I got home, I realized she was a pretty big deal in the yoga world. She's one of the most respected and well-known American yoga teachers; she has appeared on the cover of *Yoga Journal*, the industry magazine, and she conducts workshops around the world and mentors other yoga teachers. She had found the courage to share her own *not okay* publicly with thousands of people who come to her workshops and follow her work. Wasn't she afraid that everyone would judge her and just run away?

I'm sure she was afraid at first. But as she and I found out through our experiences, when we bring our real selves to the world, the world doesn't run away. I hugged Elena when she opened up. We became friends. I was reminded once again that being vulnerable doesn't isolate us; it brings us closer.

When we learn to let go of trying to achieve perfect happiness and instead compassionately embrace the reality of our lives and ourselves, we discover many deeper, kinder, and more meaningful connections within our social networks than we thought possible. I keep learning this lesson. Perhaps the most powerful reminder has been the incredible support I've received from the Happier community after I started to be more honest with them, through my happy moments and my weekly emails.

We had sent a weekly email out for a few years, sharing things like how to practice gratitude when life is challenging or ways to reduce stress through kindness. Our community loved them. About a year into my commitment to be more open about my journey, I started to write these emails myself, to make them more personal and more honest, to share ways in which I wasn't okay, as well as ways in which I found joy. The first time I did it I was freaking out: I was about to tell 250,000 people that the CEO of Happier often struggled to be happier.

I can only describe the response I got as overwhelming love. No one used the word *love*, but that is what they sent back in their emails, telling me how much my opening up had helped them to start to embrace their own feelings. This is the kind of love that we infuse into our social networks when we practice genuine acceptance, when we strengthen our ability to cultivate joy in everyday moments, and when we become courageously compassionate toward ourselves when not everything is okay. This love is not romantic, it's not the kind of love we feel for our parents or kids. It's a more universal, deeper sense of being connected to each other and experiencing the power of that connection.

"You're an unhealed healer," my teacher Janet said to me when I told her I was afraid to share my struggles because I was supposed to be the teacher, the leader, the person who was helping others become happier.

I think we're all unhealed healers. When we give up trying to find perfection or be perfect; when we embrace our lives and how we are, and within that acceptance cultivate the practice of gratitude, acceptance, intentional kindness; when we connect to our bigger why and invest in taking care of ourselves, we heal not only ourselves but also so many people around us.

So consider this my passing the baton, from one unhealed healer to another. Take what you have read in this book, practice it, make it your own. In doing so, share it with people you love, people you care about, people you work with, people you study with, people you encounter in the course of your days, and all the people who all of *those* people are connected to. You can be the force of good in the world. You can be the source of healing and of so much lasting joy.

# A Letter to My Daughter

I spent the last five years unexpectedly becoming an expert in living a happier, fuller, more meaningful life. If you had told me ten years ago that I would create a company called Happier and dedicate my life to helping people realize their greatest potential by cultivating more joy and meaning and boosting their emotional immune system, I wouldn't have believed you. I never expected that it would take me until I turned forty to find my life purpose, nor did I expect that this would be it. What I expected even less is that my life purpose would emerge out of some of my most painful struggles.

But that is the magic of becoming genuinely happier, as I've discovered. It's a journey within yourself, one that is likely to take you on a path you didn't expect. It can be difficult and at times seem impossible, but you have to keep going and learning, because it's the most worthwhile path there is.

On the eve of my fortieth birthday a few years ago, I decided to make a list of the lessons I'd learned about what it truly means to live a happier and fuller life. I love lists, and this seemed like the perfect occasion. As I was writing it, I realized that I kept thinking about my daughter, who was eleven years old at the time. I started by writing the list for myself; by the time I was in the middle of it, I was writing it for her.

What we all wish for our kids and people we care about is to be happy, healthy, fulfilled, to live a life that brings them joy and meaning. It took me a long time to realize this, but the best way we can help them do this is to do it for ourselves first. I used to think that focusing on becoming happier was selfish. I'm now certain that it's the least selfish thing I can do. In fact, I think of it as a great responsibility I have to my daughter, my family, and the people I love and care about.

So here it is, my dear readers, my list of "Forty Things I Learned about Living Happier and More Fully" (a.k.a. a letter to my daughter). I'm so grateful that you have joined me on this journey and hopeful that something I shared in this book will inspire and help you live your best life, to find more joy in everyday moments and to boost your emotional immune system so you can be okay even when things are not okay. I also hope that by sharing this list I might inspire you to create your own and share it with someone you love.

1. It's really all about love.

2. One sweater you really like is better than five sweaters you kinda sorta like and bought because they were on sale.

3. Don't wait for any one human to give you all the care and love you crave. No one can be your all, but some people can be your *a lot*. Cherish them.

4. Stop trying to be fearless. If you're trying and learning, you'll feel fear. It's okay. Remember your bigger *why*, the reason you're taking this journey, and hang on to it. It will guide you through the fear.

5. Read the entire recipe before you start cooking.

6. Be grateful for the tiniest things. They all matter. Even if you feel sad, you can find some beauty around you to appreciate. It will elevate you.

7. You deserve the gift of your own kindness. Treat yourself as you would a good friend, even when you make mistakes. It won't make you complacent; it will help you be better.

8. Most things are better after a good night of sleep.

9. Don't save your nice dishes, nice clothes, nice shoes for special occasions. Every day you're alive is a special occasion, so use the good stuff!

10. When in doubt, go for a walk.

11. You can only change yourself—not other people, not relationships, just you. If you want to change anything—including the world—start within yourself.

12. Be. Here. Now. Don't rob yourself of living today because you're lost in yesterday or leaning into tomorrow.

13. One spoonful of the real stuff is better than one cup of the low-fat stuff.

14. Happiness isn't the absence of negative emotions. You're not failing at happiness because you feel sad or angry. Let yourself feel what you feel, but don't lose sight of the little moments of warmth, kindness, or beauty that are always there, even if you have to wipe away your tears to see them.

15. Hiding your unique gifts from others isn't humility. It's stealing. True humility is to accept your responsibility to share your contributions. There may be someone whose life will be changed by them.

16. Sweat the small stuff that makes you even the tiniest bit happier. Fill your shelves with books you love. Rush to the farmers market for the season's first strawberries. Buy pens you like to write with. Move your desk to catch the morning sun. These make up the texture of your life.

17. There is no such thing as a wrong emotion. Give yourself a chance to feel what you feel, even if it's difficult. The less you try to fight or avoid a feeling you don't want to have the easier it will be to move through it.

18. You. Are. Enough. You're lovable and amazing and deserving of true genuine happiness exactly the way you are. You don't have to do anything more to earn it. You're a being, not a doing.

19. People care a lot less about what you do or how you look than you think. Mostly we're all focused on ourselves, so stop worrying about perceptions and live your life.

20. You experience 100 percent of the emotions you give to others. If you feel angry at someone, you experience anger. If you experience kindness, you feel kind.

21. It's okay to have a mess of a day. Sometimes you *do* need to eat too much, watch too much TV, and hide under the covers away from it all.

22. If you do something and it makes you feel spectacular, don't ignore that feeling. It's the universe trying to tell you: This thing you just did? Do it more often. Yes, this applies to what you do for work too.

23. Be more honest. Being vulnerable doesn't make you weak, it makes you real. Be real. It's a gift not just to yourself but to everyone around you.

24. You're not your thoughts. You're not your feelings. They're part of you but not the entirety of you. Learn to be aware of them rather than become them.

25. Make things with your hands as often as you can. Cook, paint, plant, play an instrument, anything. You'll get a break from living in your head.

26. When you're having a horrible day, even the tiniest achievements feel amazing. Clean your desk, do a handstand, write things down on your to-do list that you have already accomplished.

27. Be intentionally kind and expect nothing in return. The kindness boomerang will come back to you.

28. Give up your ideas of how something should be. Life is unfolding as it is, and you have a choice to either be awake to how it is and go from there or suffer wishing it were different.

29. Most things taste a lot better right out of the container: ice cream, milk, sardines.

30. Find time for stillness and silence every day. Don't be afraid to spend some time alone. Alone = ALL ONE.

31. The greatest moments in a friendship often come when you text a friend, "Hey, I'm feeling awful and I need you."

32. If you don't know what to do, do something. Don't wait to figure it out; start doing and you'll be able to make any decision better, later.

33. Travel more and often. This may be one of the only ways to buy happiness with money. Also, take time to travel on your own. You'll discover more about yourself than the places you visit.

34. Break your own rules as often as possible. Try spicy food even if you're "not into spicy food." Wear something bright if you usually wear black. Read things that you're normally not into. Give yourself freedom to explore.

35. Take care of yourself. It's not selfish; it's your responsibility to the people you love. There is no glory in being a martyr.

36. Laugh loudly and often.

37. Never be too busy for a hug. Or too grumpy. Or too proud.

38. Just because you can't see it right now doesn't mean the path isn't there. Keep taking steps.

39. If you have to force it—an idea, a piece of writing, a job, a relationship, a shoe—it's not meant to be. Working hard and forcing something are two different things. Learn the difference.

40. It's all really about love. Not romantic love, not any specific kind of love, just *love*. It's within you. Find it. Nurture it. Share it. Grow it. Swim in it. It's always the right answer, although sometimes you'll have a hard time seeing it. Keep looking.

# Select Bibliography

I am grateful to have benefited from the guidance of dozens of authors of wise and inspiring books as I undertook my personal journey and worked on this book. Below I have included the ones that had the greatest impact on me and those to which I specifically refer throughout this book. It is an honor to have learned from the great minds that authored them.

Coelho, Paulo, and Alan Clarke. *The Alchemist*. San Francisco: HarperOne, 2014.

Csikszentmihalyi, Mihaly. *Flow: The Psychology of Optimal Experience*. New York: Harper Perennial, 2009.

Cuddy, Amy. *Presence: Bringing Your Boldest Self to Your Biggest Challenges*. New York: Little, Brown, 2015.

David, Susan. *Emotional Agility: Get Unstuck, Embrace Change, and Thrive in Work and Life*. New York: Avery, 2016.

Doty, James R. *Into the Magic Shop: A Neurosurgeon's Quest to Discover the Mysteries of the Brain and the Secrets of the Heart*. New York: Avery, 2016.

Dyer, Wayne W. *The Power of Intention*. Carlsbad, CA: Hay House, 2005.

Emmons, Robert A. *Thanks! How the New Science of Gratitude Can Make You Happier*. New York: Houghton Mifflin, 2007.

Ferrucci, Piero. *The Power of Kindness: The Unexpected Benefits of Leading a Compassionate Life*. New York: TarcherPerigee, 2016.

Frankl, Viktor E. *Man's Search for Meaning*. Boston: Beacon Press, 2015.

Fredrickson, Barbara L. *Positivity: Groundbreaking Research Reveals How to Embrace the Hidden Strength of Positive Emotions, Overcome Negativity, and Thrive*. New York: MJF Books, 2012.

Gilbert, Daniel. *Stumbling on Happiness*. New York: Alfred A. Knopf, 2006.

Gilbert, Paul, and Choden. *Mindful Compassion: How the Science of Compassion Can Help You Understand Your Emotions, Live in the Present, and Connect Deeply with Others.* Oakland, CA: New Harbinger Publications, 2014.

Grant, Adam. *Give and Take: A Revolutionary Approach to Success.* New York: Penguin Random House, 2013.

Kabat-Zinn, Jon. *Wherever You Go, There You Are: Mindfulness Meditation in Everyday Life.* New York: Hyperion, 2009.

Korb, Alex. *The Upward Spiral: Using Neuroscience to Reverse the Course of Depression, One Small Change at a Time.* Oakland, CA: New Harbinger Publications, 2015.

Neff, Kristin. *Self-Compassion: The Proven Power of Being Kind to Yourself.* New York: William Morrow, 2015.

Palmer, Amanda. *The Art of Asking: How I Learned to Stop Worrying and Let People Help.* New York: Grand Central Publishing, 2015.

Ram Dass. *Be Here Now, Remember.* San Cristobal, NM: Lama Foundation, 1987.

Ram Dass, and Rameshwar Das. *Polishing the Mirror: How to Live from Your Spiritual Heart.* Louisville, CO: Sounds True, 2014.

Salzberg, Sharon. *Lovingkindness: The Revolutionary Art of Happiness.* Boulder, CO: Shambhala, 2002.

Sandberg, Sheryl, and Adam Grant. *Option B: Facing Adversity, Building Resilience, and Finding Joy.* New York: Alfred A. Knopf, 2017.

Seligman, Martin E. P. *Flourish: A Visionary New Understanding of Happiness and Well-Being.* New York: Atria, 2013.

Singer, Michael A. *The Surrender Experiment: My Journey into Life's Perfection.* New York: Harmony Books, 2015.

———. *The Untethered Soul: The Journey beyond Yourself.* Oakland, CA: New Harbinger Publications, 2008.

Stryker, Rod. *The Four Desires: Creating a Life of Purpose, Happiness, Prosperity, and Freedom.* New York: Delacorte Press, 2011.

Tolle, Eckhart. *The Power of Now.* Vancouver, BC: Namaste, 2007.

# About the Author

Nataly Kogan is an entrepreneur, speaker, and author on a mission to help millions of people cultivate their happier skills by making simple, scientifically backed practices part of their daily life.

Nataly immigrated to the United States as a refugee from the former Soviet Union when she was thirteen years old. Starting her journey in the projects outside of Detroit, Nataly reached the highest level of corporate success, including careers at McKinsey and Microsoft, and became a venture capitalist at the age of twenty-six. But she found herself unfulfilled and was inspired to learn how to live a truly happier, fuller life.

Her discoveries and explorations in scientific research and Eastern disciplines, including yoga and Buddhism, led her to create Happier, a company whose award-winning mobile application, online courses, and Happier at Work training programs have helped hundreds of thousands of people improve their emotional health.

Nataly is a sought-out keynote speaker and has appeared in hundreds of media publications. She is a self-taught abstract artist, a devoted yogi, and lover of all things striped. But what brings her the greatest joy is spending time with her family, including her husband, Avi, and daughter, Mia. Together, they live outside of Boston, although Nataly will always be a New Yorker at heart.

To bring Nataly to your company or organization, please email speaking@happier.com. Please visit happier.com to sign up for Nataly's weekly email newsletter and to explore many helpful resources, including short videos, online courses, information about workshops, and more.

# About Sounds True

Sounds True is a multimedia publisher whose mission is to inspire and support personal transformation and spiritual awakening. Founded in 1985 and located in Boulder, Colorado, we work with many of the leading spiritual teachers, thinkers, healers, and visionary artists of our time. We strive with every title to preserve the essential "living wisdom" of the author or artist. It is our goal to create products that not only provide information to a reader or listener, but that also embody the quality of a wisdom transmission.

For those seeking genuine transformation, Sounds True is your trusted partner. At SoundsTrue.com you will find a wealth of free resources to support your journey, including exclusive weekly audio interviews, free downloads, interactive learning tools, and other special savings on all our titles.

To learn more, please visit SoundsTrue.com/freegifts or call us toll-free at 800.333.9185.

SOUNDS TRUE
many voices, one journey